REAL ESTATE SIDE HUSTLE FOR INVESTORS

By Phil Wong

RESULTS PRESS

Results Press
Unit 229
#180, 8601 Lincoln Blvd.
Los Angeles, California 90045

www.theresultspress.com

ISBN-13: 978-0-9988905-9-3

First Edition

Copyright © 2020 by Phil Wong

All rights reserved. No part of this book may be reproduced in any form without the prior writer permission from the publisher. The opinions and conclusions drawn in this book are solely those of the author. The author and publisher bear no liability in connection with the use of the ideas presented.

- - -

Foreword

Over the years I have worked, partnered, and met with a lot of incredible individuals, including Phil Wong. I've known Phil for years and I was lucky enough to be there when he started his real estate investing journey--and what a journey it's been. Maintaining and growing a real estate portfolio can be a struggle enough on its own, but the trials and tribulations Phil went through to get this book out, to share his passion and the aforementioned struggles and lessons he has learned along the way is a story unto itself. That being said, I'm honoured to be writing these words, the first words of many that will open your mind and expand your life.

Having worked with Phil over the years, I have seen great growth and transformation, from someone starting out in real estate, to someone who inspires, teaches and motivates others. He took the steps to make things happen, and in doing so, he is showing others how to walk this same path so that they too can reach their goals.

Real estate is a powerful thing. If you look throughout history, the most successful organizations, families and individuals derived a large portion of their success from real estate. I, for one, can tell you that real estate has changed my life for the better--and not just monetarily. Real estate has opened doors, allowing me to meet amazing people like Phil, presenting me with opportunities I could hardly imagine a decade ago and most importantly, it has afforded me *time*. Time to do the things I really love in life, such as spend time with my family, friends and live my passions. It has also allowed me to add value and impact other people's lives as much and as often as I can. Another vital element real estate has provided me are choices. The choice to teach, the choice to write, the choice to travel, the choice to build relationships, and other endless choices!

Real estate is a long journey, but I'm happy to say this book will give you plenty of fuel to get started--tips, steps and guidelines so you can start off on the right foot. When you have someone like Phil in your back pocket, having this book as a resource to tap into time and time again, you are bound to find success quickly and with peace of mind. I'm happy I can take these first steps with you.

If you are ready to take action and change your life forever, dive into this book and enjoy the adventure upon which you are about to go.

Remember...TODAY is the day to UNLOCK your POTENTIAL.

Kindest regards,

Fong Chua
Best-selling author, Business Strategist, Entrepreneur, Coach and Speaker

Fong Chua's mission is to add value to as many people's lives as he can. Leveraging the skills he has learned from his coaches and over the years, he has emceed charity events, hosted business workshops and spoken on stages in Canada and USA. He has helped others become bestselling authors, interviewed the likes of Olympic Champion Bruni Surin and Celebrity Apprentice George Ross, and shared a panel with Shark Tank's Kevin Harrington. To find out more about Fong Chua, visit meetfongchua.com.

About the Author

Phil was born and raised in Edmonton, Alberta and graduated with dual degrees in Biological Sciences and Pharmacy from the University of Alberta in 2011. His love for the mountains convinced him to move to Calgary in 2016, where he currently resides.

Phil has a passion for travelling and loves pushing the limits of his mind and body. Having been to 31 countries and being an accomplished triathlete, marathoner, rock climber and martial artist, Phil has since focused his passion and drive to the realm of real estate investing.

Realizing that real estate was the ideal vehicle for him to build his wealth while still allowing time for friends, family and living the active lifestyle that he enjoys, Phil began to actively pursue investments in this area with great results.

Seeing the life-changing potential of his investments, he has gotten into the business of helping others achieve their financial and life goals through mentoring, coaching, and joint venture partnerships in real estate investments.

Phil and his partners have created an educational platform for Canadian real estate investors with a goal to make real estate less scary for the average investor. More info about this can be found on www.cwho.ca.

In his free time, Phil can be found exploring mountains or training for his next race.

Dedication

I'd like to dedicate this to my parents Don and Julie, my sister Diana, my partner-in-crime Krystyna and all my friends who've supported me (you know who you are). I couldn't have done this without any of you.

CONTENTS

Foreword 3

INTRODUCTION 13

CHAPTER 1 – MINDSET 14

    Why Do You Want to Invest in Real Estate?   17
    Are You Prepared to do the Work Required?   17
    Don't Fall for It   18
    Find Your Niche   19
    Stumbling upon Real Estate   19
    Next Actionable Step   22

CHAPTER 2 – GETTING YOUR FINANCIAL SHIT IN ORDER 23

    Get a Handle on Your Debt   23
    Pay Yourself First   27
    Create a Budget   27
    Make a Goal and Crush It   28
    Living like a Student   28
    Next Actionable Step   30

CHAPTER 3 – EDUCATION 31

    Books   31
    Investment Courses   32
    Join a Real-Estate Investment Group/Association   32
    Hire a Real-Estate Coach   33
    Educating Myself   33
    Next Actionable Step   35

CHAPTER 4 – YOUR REAL ESTATE TEAM 36

Realtor	37
Mortgage Broker	38
Lawyer	38
Bookkeeper	39
Accountant	39
Property Manager	40
Treat Your Investment as a Business	41
How I Built My Power Team	41
Next Actionable Step	42

CHAPTER 5 - TENANT AND PROPERTY PROFILING 43

Tenant Profile	45
Tenant Avatar	46
Don't Just Look at Price	49
How I Found My Niche	50
Next Actionable Step	51

CHAPTER 6 – PROPERTY ANALYSIS 52

GDP Growth	53
Job Prospects	53
Major Employers in the Area	54
Population Growth	54
Property Analysis	55
Researching Rents	55
Expenses	56
Reserve Fund	59
Gross and Total Debt Service Ratios	59
Cashflow: How Much is Enough?	61
Analysis Paralysis	63
Next Actionable Step	64

CHAPTER 7 – FINDING YOUR FIRST INVESTMENT 65

How I Find My Properties	66
Next Actionable Step	67

CHAPTER 8 – PURCHASE AND NEGOTIATION 68

Knowing What You Want — 70
Pressure Points — 71
Financing and Conditions — 72
My Experience with Purchase and Negotiations — 76
Next Actionable Step — 78

CHAPTER 9 – MARKETING FOR TENANTS 80

Pricing the Rent Right — 81
Writing a Good Advertisement — 82
Compelling Visuals — 84
Tenant Screening — 85
Tenant Screening Checklist — 85
Moving Tenants In — 91
My Experience with Finding Tenants — 91
Next Actionable Step — 92

CHAPTER 10 – TENANT MANAGEMENT 93

To Manage or Not to Manage (Yourself) — 95
When to Hire Out Management — 95
Build Rapport with Your Tenants — 96
Keeping the Good Ones — 97
Getting Rid of the Bad Apples — 98
Managing My Tenants — 99
Next Actionable Step — 100

CHAPTER 11 – JOINT VENTURES 101

My Growth Story — 103
Next Actionable Step — 105

CHAPTER 12 – TREATING IT LIKE A BUSINESS 106

Systems — 108
Scaling or Scalability — 109
Be a Professional — 111

My Systems and Processes 112
Next Actionable Step 113

CHAPTER 13 – WHAT IF… 114

What if the Tenants Don't Pay? 115
What if My Tenant Trashes the Property? 115
What if the Property Doesn't Rent? 115
What if the Housing Market Drops? 116
What if Interest Rates go Up? 116
What if Rent Control gets Implemented? 117
What if My Rent Doesn't Cover My Expenses? 117
What if the Property Ends Up Vacant for Several
Months Between Tenants? 117
What if Different Tenants in a Property don't get Along? 118

CHAPTER 14 – BRINGING IT ALL TOGETHER 120

Next Actionable Step 122

Phil Wong

INTRODUCTION

When I started my real estate investing journey, I felt lost, clueless and thoroughly intimidated by what lay ahead of me. Although I had help from my dad, who had some experience in real estate, my real fear came from what I didn't know. As of writing this book, I'm seven years into my real-estate investing journey and I feel as if I've achieved some modicum of success. At the very least, I still have friends, my family still loves me and my finances haven't imploded. I'm calling that a win!

However, I've made a ton of mistakes along the way, and have felt like an idiot more times than I can count. So, I decided to write this book in the hopes I can help some new real estate investors avoid some of the hurdles upon which I tripped...and subsequently faceplanted.

At any real-estate investment or motivational seminar, only about 5% of the people in the audience will take action in response to what they've learned. In fact, one of the things which kept me from moving ahead earlier in my career was that I didn't know what to do next. As a result, at the end of every chapter I've included a Next Actionable Step to move you forward. At the very least, I'm hoping this book will inspire you to do one thing that moves you closer to your goals and your dreams.

— Phil Wong February 2020

CHAPTER 1
MINDSET

Dave wakes up to the sound of his vibrating cell phone on his bedside table. He blearily looks at his alarm clock. It's 7:00 a.m.

"What the hell," he mutters. He glances at the Caller ID display on his phone. It's his tenant--again. He lets it go to voicemail.

Last year, Dave's wife Melinda talked him into buying a rental property as an investment. They were both in their mid-thirties at the time with decent jobs, no kids and they had some money saved up in both of their RRSPs for retirement. Dave thought they were on a decent path for a secure future, but after talking to her friend who owned a couple of real-estate investment properties, Melinda became convinced this was the only way to retire early and get out of the rat race. Dave was reluctant, but he went with it anyway, and ever since it has been nothing but headaches.

Listening to the voicemail his tenant left, it turns out the fridge at the rental property broke again. This is the second time this year, and last time it cost $500 to fix. Now they have to pay to fix it again and it's eating up what little cashflow they had saved up from the rental property. Dave feels as if all this property does is eat up their money and time with nothing to show for it. It's yet another thing to deal with, tacked onto a never- ending list of tenant complaints. Now, Dave gets chills every time his phone rings, fearing it's his tenant calling about another issue.

Melinda had made it sound as if it would be easy money--buy a house, get someone to rent it and get paid every month.

Done.

Either Melinda didn't know what she was talking about or she'd lied, because this endeavor is anything but easy. From the stress and anxiety of carrying two mortgage payments while looking for a renter, running around doing showings at all hours of the day, to making sure the prospects weren't serial killers, it felt like more work than either of them had ever wanted or asked for. Dave constantly feels stressed and overwhelmed—and for what? To retire a couple of years earlier after still working for a lifetime, anyway?

Is this all even worth it?

Dave grumpily drags his ass out of bed to get ready for work and another long day.

Well, that was a little ball of sunshine, wasn't it? How about we replay that again, but this time with a slight shift in perspective?

Dave wakes up to the sound of his vibrating cell phone on his bedside table. Looking at his phone, he sees it's his tenant. He snatches up the phone and says, "Oh damn, that sucks. Well, thanks for letting me know, Vince. I'll make some calls today and get that fridge fixed for you. Thanks. Bye."

He glances at his alarm clock. 7:00 a.m. It's time to wake up for work, anyway. Good timing. Dave and Melinda had decided to get into their first real-estate investment last year, so they bought a little townhouse and rented it out. This is the second time the fridge has broken in as many years, so that's been annoying, but aside from that and a couple of other issues, so far, so good. Dave and Melinda are both in their mid-thirties with no kids yet, and they have some money saved up. Melinda has a friend who does real-estate investing and it seemed to be working well for her, so Melinda and Dave had a discussion and decided to go for it too. The rent covers the cost of the property with a couple hundred bucks left over. Not amazing, but the mortgage is being paid down and the cashflow is enough to build a little reserve fund for emergencies just like this. Not a nickel comes out of Dave and Melinda's personal pockets.

In truth, it was harder than they'd originally imagined to get everything up and running for the rental property. Taking time to show the property and screening the tenants was a bit of work, but once they had found someone they liked, it was just a matter of a few phone calls and emails here and there. The rest of the time, they just got paid. Now they get $9,000 paid into the principle of their mortgage every year, plus another $2,500 a year in cashflow. Not bad for working hard one month of the year. By the time they're fifty-years-old, the house will be paid off and it's all gravy from there.

The point of these two stories is what a huge difference mindset, and your perspective as a result of that mindset, can make. Dave and Melinda are dealing with the same problems in both stories, but focusing on the bigger picture and knowing what they're working for makes all the difference in the world. Whether you already have a few investment properties or you're just starting out, it's worthwhile for you to ask yourself the following questions to make sure you're on the right track and haven't lost your way.

Why Do You Want to Invest in Real Estate?

This is probably one of the biggest questions. What is your ultimate goal? What is it that drives you? Do you want to live a limitless life? Retire early? What is your *why*? I ask this because you will come on some hard times if you spend enough time investing in real estate. I can guarantee it. If you don't have a good reason for doing it, you may very well give up at the moment when you most need to push through.

Are You Prepared to do the Work Required?

HGTV and their plethora of home renovation shows has made investing in real estate look very easy. Knock down a wall, add new flooring, a new kitchen, slap on a coat of paint and voila!
You've got yourself an amazing home people will practically trip over to bid on. Then there are all the real estate

workshops that promise you an easy way to make bucketloads of money for very little work. For a small fee of your life savings and your first-born child, they promise to show you the secrets of how you too can make a fortune in real estate, then take pictures of yourself on a yacht full of attractive people.

Don't Fall for It

Real estate investing isn't as much work in the traditional sense compared to a full-time job, but it's not a small amount of work, either. Between sourcing the properties to marketing for tenants, showing the homes, screening your tenants and then managing your tenants while they are residents can be a daunting job, especially if you have full-time employment and a family on top of that. There are also the emotional and financial stresses of considering the amount of money invested and having to carry more than one mortgage. There are some rough days for sure. They do pass however, and things will get better – until it happens again. The bottom line is it can be a grind, so don't fool yourself into thinking it's all going to be sunshine and roses.

Take your time and ponder those questions for a bit. In the meantime, let's move on. Many people who start real estate investing read books and attend seminars and become inundated with information. The result of this is what I like to call the *Shiny Object Syndrome*--or *SOS*, for short. People with *SOS* get drawn into every new real estate tactic they come across.

Everything sounds awesome and they want to learn it all and implement everything. Every investor experiences this in the beginning, so it's nothing to be ashamed of. Some tactics are actually pretty awesome. Perhaps you find and secure under contract a property for below market-price and then sell the contract to another investor for $10,000 with no cost to you and only a couple of hours of work. Who doesn't want that? If that works for you, then great, but not everyone has the skillset to pull off something like that on a regular basis. In addition, not everyone has the time to do everything--which brings us to our next point.

Find Your Niche

Discover your strengths and focus on them. Find out what type of investing you'd prefer and focus on that. Some of the greatest investors in the world aren't great because they have no weaknesses, they're great because they know their strengths and find situations where the game is stacked in their favor. You should be no different. Let's face it--you're not going to be able to do everything, or at least not everything *well*, so why not just find one or two areas you're really good at and just kill it? For example, if you're good at renovations and don't have a lot of money, then a *fix and flip* might be a good strategy for you. On the other hand, if you have a lot of capital and don't want to do a lot of work, then *buy and hold* is a good choice. As much as Happy Gilmore wanted to play hockey, golf was his game. Find your game and take it home.

Stumbling upon Real Estate

My family has a little history in real estate. When my parents first arrived in Edmonton, Canada in the '80s from Vietnam, the only thing they owned were the clothes on their backs. Coming from a war-torn country where a Communist government had just taken over a decade earlier, they had all their possessions confiscated and came to Canada hoping for a better life. My parents had my sister and me shortly after their arrival. They worked hard to provide for us, often working seven days a week while my grandparents took care of us. My dad had a plan, though, and buying a home for his family was one of the first things on the list. He saw renting as a waste of money, and he had us in our own house within a couple of years. We slowly upgraded homes over the next 20 years, but it wasn't until my dad was 50 years old that he began real estate investing in earnest. In 2006, he combined funds with a couple of friends.

Within four years, he had accumulated a portfolio of over 40 doors. Eight years later, my dad and his business partners liquidated their portfolio and retired at the comfortable age of 60.

I was just a dumb-ass kid going through university at the time, so I didn't realize what a big deal that was. Real estate was just some ephemeral thing my dad did on the side while working at his factory job six days a week. A couple of years after graduation and after coming across a good deal on a new build, my dad convinced me to purchase my own place in Edmonton. At the time, I was living in Canmore for work, but I believed I would be back in Edmonton before long, so I put down a deposit and forgot about it for a while. When the house was finished, I realized I loved the mountains and didn't want to move back. In any case, after a few months of paying both rent at my new place in Canmore in addition to my mortgage, I recognized how quickly I was going broke, so I reluctantly rented out my place in Edmonton.

But then suddenly the rent on my house yielded me $400 a month in cashflow and I was like, "Holy shit, this is awesome!" At that point, this light bulb turned on in my brain and I realized I could make some money off this real estate investing thing. I then read like crazy, joined the Real

Estate Investment Network and learned as much as I could on the subject. I even divested most of my stock holdings and shovelled them into real estate.

I like real estate for a few reasons. One is that it provides passive income. My *why* is to live a life where I can travel the world with my loved ones with no reservations, and that passive income provides me with this opportunity. Secondly, real estate is a business where you can set up a system to run it and then be outside that system. What I mean by that is you don't have to be a cog in the machine. You can hire property managers, accountants, lawyers, etc. and they will help you with everything you need to run the property without having to deal with the day-to-day. I can feel pretty lazy sometimes and the idea of eventually not working as much but still generating a decent income is an appealing proposition.

To further my lazy ambitions, I've focused on investing in new builds, which means there are less things that break down and must be fixed, as well as attracting well-paying tenants who love the place and don't bother me for the most part. It's awesome. I highly recommend this method for first-time investors because it's just plain easy. You'll know your costs going in and if you've done your research properly, you'll have a good idea what you'll be making in monthly rent (more on this in Chapter 7). Manage it well and you'll be in good shape.

Everyone has their own preferences, but that's the beauty of real estate. You can invest in whatever it is that fits your personality. Want to be hands-on? Get a *fix and flip*. Want zero work? Be a *money partner*. It's better than the donut selection at Tim Horton's.

Next Actionable Step

WRITE DOWN the reason you want to invest in real estate and put it somewhere you'll see it every day. By writing it down, it makes it real, not just some random idea in your head. And by putting it where you'll see it, it'll keep reminding you of why you're doing this. This is especially important when things get tough--and things will get tough. Keep your head down and keep your *why* in mind. Work the problem and you'll get through it.

CHAPTER 2

GETTING YOUR FINANCIAL SHIT IN ORDER

If you've ever listened to the safety announcement on a flight, they tell you ad nauseum to always put the oxygen mask on yourself first before helping others. It makes sense, because if you're a blue, asphyxiated mess, you're not going to be very useful to anyone else. Well, this is the chapter that makes sure you have your metaphorical oxygen mask on before you go balls-to-the-wall into real estate investing. It's important to have all your financials in order so you don't build your real estate empire on a crappy foundation and have the whole thing implode on you, leaving a giant sinkhole where your life used to be.

Get a Handle on Your Debt

There are different schools of thought on this subject.

There's a debate regarding whether there is such thing as good debt versus bad debt or whether ALL debt should be avoided like the plague. This war will likely wage on forever. For the sake of this book and the whole concept of real estate investing in general, let's go with the notion that there is such a thing as good and bad debt. A fundamental point behind real estate investing is you can leverage the money you have to purchase an asset that's worth several times more than your cash-on-hand. Without that, real estate investing would not be nearly as profitable, and frankly, not worthwhile.

So, with that being said, GOOD DEBT is debt you incur to purchase an asset that will generate an income or appreciate in value (ideally both), enabling you to (ideally) outpace the interest you have to pay on that debt. In other words, you use the money to buy something which generates more money than you lose.

A good use of debt is when you purchase a property that still generates positive cashflow after paying off the principal, interest, taxes, and insurance. For example, Melissa buys a property for $300,000 with a 20% down payment, which means she puts up $60,000 herself and the bank loans her $240,000 for the rest. Every month, she pays $1,500, which includes her mortgage, property taxes and insurance. She rents the house for $1,800 and makes a tidy $300 of positive cashflow per month from it. Not only is she making money on the principal paydown of the mortgage and the cashflow every month, but as long as she has a down payment, she can support an infinite number of these properties because she doesn't have to owe any money every month.

A not-so-good example is if you buy a house that has *negative* cash flow but you think will appreciate more than the interest you're paying over time. Use the same example as above, but this time, the market will only support a rental rate of $1,200 a month instead of $1,800. Melissa now has to pitch in $300 from her own pocket every month to keep this investment from going under. In this case, she can pray the appreciation might outpace the interest rate and net her a profit in the end, but she's really speculating (aka gambling) on that hope. Although this wouldn't strictly be classified as bad debt as she's still making some money on the mortgage paydown, it's not the best use of leveraged money. Furthermore, how many of these properties can Melissa support if she has to pay $300 into each one every month? Probably a lot less than infinity.

Actual BAD DEBT, on the other hand, is when you borrow money to purchase something which depreciates in value. Here, not only are you losing money in the form of interest which you will never get back, but the worst part is the thing you bought is losing value every second you own it. One example is a car--or even worse, consumer debt. With a car, at least sometimes you get great financing rates (as low as 0%) and it's something you actually need to get to work to make money. If this is the case for you, look for a used car at a dealership. At least you won't lose 25% of the value as soon as you drive it off the lot, as is the case with a new one. If you're one of those people who is carrying around credit card debt at 19.99% or more and think that's okay, put down this book and find yourself a credit counsellor right now.

If you can't live within your means and have a healthy savings account, saving up for a house down payment is probably the least of your worries.

"But Phil, I've read all I can get my hands on about real estate investing and I can leverage my knowledge to attract investors. I don't need my own money!"

It's good that you're so optimistic, as I believe that's one of the prerequisites of being an entrepreneur but think about it for second. If *you* were the investor, would you give money to someone who has no track record? Moreover, would you give money to someone who has no track record, is living paycheque to paycheque and clearly doesn't have their financial shit together?

Exactly. So, help yourself before you help others and be the example others can emulate.

Now, some people may have debt where the interest rate is so low, they think by putting money into an investment, will likely generate a higher return. Debt in this category usually applies to student loans, some low-interest car loans, a mortgage, or even a home equity line of credit (HELOC).

You can use this online calculator at http://www.calcxml.com/calculators/pay-off-debt-or-invest to input the interest rate on your debt versus the expected return you will get from an investment and see where the best place is to put your hard-earned moolah. Generally speaking, if you're young and interest rates are low, you should pay the minimum on the loan and put money into an investment with a high rate of return to take advantage of the power of compound interest. However, if you're closer to retirement, then paying off the debt first may be a better plan. Everybody's situation is different, so sitting down with a financial planner to figure out the best use of your money might be a good way to start planning your investment career.

Pay Yourself First

This is an age-old adage in personal finance, but it never gets old. Whenever you get paid, before you do anything else with that money, *pay yourself first*. A good rule of thumb is to pay yourself 20% of your gross monthly income and save it or invest it, then live off the remaining 80%. If you're one who lacks self-control, you can set up automatic deductions from your bank account, or even better, directly from your paycheque. You'll never see it and you'd be surprised how little you miss it after a while. Remember, wealth is not how much you make, but how much you keep.

Create a Budget

It won't do you much good if you frivolously spend the remaining 80% of your paycheque and end up racking up more debt than you can pay off in a month. This is where a budget comes in. If you already have a budget, great. If you're like some others who have a budget but can never stick to it, then some rewards or punishments for achieving or not achieving your goals may be a good motivation. If you have no idea even where to start, then keep reading.

The first step is to know where all your money is going, so you have to track your spending. You can track it using an app, an Excel spreadsheet, or even pen and paper if that's what works for you. For those who are a little more tech-savvy, you can use programs like Mint.com or YNAB (You Need a Budget) to track your spending for you. These programs allow you to link all your various accounts, such as your chequing, savings, credit cards, etc. so you can see it all in one place. Every time you spend somewhere, you will see it show up and count against the budget you've set for yourself. After a couple months of tracking your spending, you will have a better idea of where your money goes. Then you can set a limit as to how much you'll spend in each category, such as groceries, eating out, entertainment, etc. and do your best to stick within those limits.

It's tougher than it sounds. You'll probably go over budget here and there, and you may have to make some sacrifices. There will come a time when you'll have to decide between a night out with friends or future financial security. If you decide on a night out, you'll have to give up something else in your budget. Just stick to it and you'll eventually get the hang of it.

Make a Goal and Crush It

Now that you've paid off your bad debt, have started putting money aside and are living below your means, it's time to make a savings goal for yourself. Doing something without focus rarely gets a person very far. Having an end goal you can see and on which you can focus is what drives a person to succeed. The question now comes down to how much house do you want to buy? Say you want a $300,000 house. A 5% down payment will be $15,000 (assuming this is your first house; a second property may require 20%). Now your one job is to save that $15,000. Sell your car and take public transit. Pick up another job. Pack more lunches. Give up that damned daily latte. Do whatever you have to do to make that $15,000 a reality. How soon you get there just comes down to how badly you want it.

Living like a Student

When I got my first job after graduating from university, I knew *nothing* about personal finance or investing. In my opinion, one way in which our educational system fails us is how little it prepares us for real life--but that's a discussion for another time. Getting thrown into real life was actually a shock for me. I had the benefit of attending school in my hometown of Edmonton, Alberta, so I was lucky enough to live at home the whole time. I moved out right after graduation, and what a wake-up call that was. Fortunately, it wasn't my first job, and I knew better than to blow all my money on video games, movies and nights out at the bar. But when it came to setting a budget, dealing with bills, and investing my money, I had no clue.

Money was never a taboo topic in my household when I was growing up. My parents did well financially, but the only bit of wisdom I seemed to walk away with was never to owe credit card debt. For some reason, everything else fell by the wayside. In any case, I dove hard into personal finance and read everything I could get my hands on. Books I thought were awesome included **Rich Dad, Poor Dad** by Robert Kiyosaki, **The Wealthy Barber Returns** by David Chilton, **The Richest Man in Babylon** by George S. Clason and **The Millionaire Next Door** by Thomas J. Stanley and William D. Danko. I even subscribed to *Moneysense* magazine for a few years.

Along the way, I figured out all my expenses and set up an automatic transfer of $500 a month to a savings account. Anything left over at the end of the month would also go into the account. I never bought any new furniture, made all my own lunches and coffee every day and bought a used car which I learned how to maintain myself. Essentially, I continued to live the poor student lifestyle which I was already accustomed to, and after three years, I had finally saved enough to put a down payment on my first home. It finally made all those batches of spaghetti lunches and dinners worthwhile…sort of.

Next Actionable Step

This one is simple but not easy. Start saving. Your first step is to decide how much to save and set up an automatic transfer to your savings account, so you don't even see it. Then start tracking your expenses and create a budget with the money you have left. Cut expenses, get a part-time job and do what you can to get that down-payment for your first property. It may suck for a while, but your future self will thank you for it.

CHAPTER 3
EDUCATION

When it comes to *buy and holds*, real estate investing is simple, but not the easiest thing in the world. There's still a lot to learn in order to make sure you don't screw yourself over along the way. The devil's in the details.

Fortunately, there are a ton of ways to educate yourself in real estate that will fit with any learning style.

Books

It may be obvious if you're reading this, but books are a great resource for everything real estate. There are enough books written about this subject that you can pretty much find one fitting any niche for which you're looking. The one drawback I find is a lot of books focus on
U.S. real estate, which may not be applicable to the Canadian market. Just make sure the book covers your home market before you decide to purchase it. If you don't like

reading, audiobooks are a great alternative, especially if you drive a lot.

Investment Courses

There are courses out there which offer great information at a reasonable price, but there are also ones which--how do I put this delicately--bleed you out and then hang you out to dry. The ones I'm talking about are those free or low-cost weekend courses which offer you a peek behind the curtain but then upsell you a $15,000 course if you want to learn more. That money can be better spent in a hundred ways, so don't get duped into buying these expensive courses.

If you ask around, you will likely find some real estate groups around your city hosting monthly workshops to educate investors. The best part is many of these workshops cost very little to attend.

If you're looking for something bigger but still affordable, the Real Estate Intelligence Network (REIN) or Commonwealth Home Ownership (CWHO) offers regular weekend courses in real estate investing that is crammed full of valuable information.

Join a Real-Estate Investment Group/Association

Google *real estate investment group (your city)* and I'm sure you'll find a number of groups where real estate investors meet on a regular basis. These places are a great way to network with other investors and pick their brains to get an idea of what other investors in your area do. They're also a great way to get referrals to build up your professional team (more on this in Chapter 4) and some even invite guest speakers to give presentations on certain areas of real estate investing. If you're actively investing, joining a group like this is probably one of the best things you can do to accelerate your growth. One of the largest groups in Canada is the Real Estate Intelligence Network (REIN), which holds monthly meetings in multiple cities across the country. Commonwealth Home Ownership is another great group to join for those living in Alberta who want a more customized, hands-on approach to real estate investing that generates real results.

Hire a Real-Estate Coach

A good coach can be worth every nickel and more if you're serious about getting your real estate investing off the ground. Not only are they a wealth of information, but they can guide you around all the pitfalls they encountered early in their careers. You have someone dedicated to ensuring you're on the best path, checking your deals and most importantly, keeping your ass accountable and moving forward. Many coaches specialize in their own style of investing, so make sure that the coach you choose has a style which is in line with yours.

Educating Myself

I had bought two investment properties a year prior to finding out about REIN, and let's just say I am very grateful I found real estate group to join before I went any further. I had not yet made any catastrophic mistakes, and I understood enough math to know I had to make more money from the rent than I had in expenses, but otherwise, I knew nothing about real estate investing. In short--so far, I had lucked out. Truth be told, I didn't know I even *needed* more education. Thinking back on it now, that was crazy naïve thinking.

I started off by attending the REIN weekend ACRE event, which stands for Authentic Canadian Real Estate. It's a weekend crash course in everything real estate investing, with a heavier focus on *buy-and-holds*, as that is how most investors get started. That weekend blew my mind.

You know the line from Disney's Pocahontas, "You'll learn things you never knew you never knew?" Well, that was me. It also opened my eyes to the full potential of real estate. I always thought if I could get myself two-to-three properties then I'd be set for retirement, but I met people who had hundreds of properties and were living lives of which I could only dream.

Before 1954, no one could run a four-minute mile. People had tried for decades with no success and the world started believing it was a threshold which couldn't be surpassed by the human body--that the human body was physically incapable of moving that fast. Then along came Roger Bannister (now Sir Roger Bannister), a medical student with a passion for running. On May 6, 1954, for the first time in history, he crushed it by running a mile in 3:59.4. Only 46 days later, John Landy, an Australian runner, broke the record again by running a mile in 3:58.0. One year later, three runners broke this record in a *single race!*

Most barriers in our lives are the ones we erect for ourselves, and what attending REIN and other workshops did for me was, as I learned more from others about what could be done -- what *had already been done* -- it broke down barrier after barrier for me. With this new insight, I blew past the three-property mark in my second year of investing and haven't looked back since.

In addition to the workshops and seminars I took, I read a *lot*. I also listened to a ton of podcasts and pretty much consumed everything I could get my hands on. A word of warning: it's during this period of knowledge consumption that the symptoms of *SOS* will begin to manifest itself. For a while, I wanted to do everything. *Rent-to-owns, agreements-for-sale, fix- and-flips*--you name it, I was down.

I started asking more experienced investors for advice and got the same line over and over. Focus on one niche and do it well. Hell, do it until you're bored with it. That's when you know you're getting good.

So that's what I did. I focused primarily on new, purpose-built suited houses and I couldn't be happier.

Next Actionable Step

Look up real-estate investment groups or meetups in your area and go check them out. The point here is to meet other real-estate investors in your area to build your network and pick their brains. It's amazing what talking to a few other investors can do for your investing career. Get off your ass and make some new friends. If you're not a very social person, make some acquaintances.

Just get out there!

CHAPTER 4

YOUR REAL ESTATE TEAM

I think we can all agree Tony Stark, a.k.a. *Iron Man*, is pretty awesome. Genius billionaire philanthropist with a high-tech flying suit who can take on a small army. As awesome as he is, he's still just one guy, and when fending off otherworldly threats or an army of killer robots, he needs a team to help him out.

The beautiful thing about the Avengers is they all have unique strengths. These strengths make the team stronger than any one of them could be on their own. Captain America's great combat skills, tactical sense and super-strength make him a great leader and frontline soldier. The Hulk is a giant, green rage monster who can take on even the biggest threats. Thor is damned near invincible and can summon lightning to destroy large swaths of enemies. Black

Widow is a master spy who is an expert at extracting information from others. Lastly, Hawkeye can shoot arrows really well...

The point is, they're stronger together than when any of them are alone--and not pointing any fingers, but some of them definitely need a team more than others *cough*...Hawkeye...*cough.** If even Tony Stark needs a team, then so do you.

Real estate investors oftentimes feel like lone wolves. You're out there knocking on doors, finding partners and putting together deals, oftentimes by yourself. Your family and friends may think you're crazy or brave or little bit of both, and they might support you, but the hustle is all you. Despite all this, real estate investing is still a team sport. You have to find the deals, transact those deals, manage the properties and deal with the finances. This is where building a team comes in.

You need Realtors, lawyers, property managers and accountants, whether you want them or not. If you're only planning on buying one or two properties, then having a great team may not matter as much, but if you plan to grow your real estate portfolio, then having a solid, consistent team is essential to success.

Let's take a look at what some of these team members can do for you.

Realtor

When most people think of real estate, Realtors are the first experts who come to mind, and rightly so, as oftentimes they are the first step in any real estate transaction. You can sometimes get by without using one for private sales and *For-Sale-by-Owner* (FSBO) listings, but a good Realtor can help you narrow down what you're looking for and save you a ton of time.

It is important you find a Realtor who understands investment real estate, and ideally is an investor themselves. From saving you time, to running comparables and being your eyes and ears in the market, a good, investment-focused Realtor is indispensable for an investor looking to grow their portfolio in the long-term.

Mortgage Broker

Almost every real estate purchase requires financing, and that's where a mortgage broker comes in. Why shop around for rates yourself when you can have someone more qualified do it for you? And the best part? It's free! The brokers get a commission from the lending institution to which they refer you, and as an added bonus, you only have to get your credit checked once, rather than several times at different institutions if you're shopping around yourself, limiting the hits to your credit score. Ideally, your broker should also be familiar with working with investors. By sharing your investment strategy with your broker, you can structure your financing in the best way to reach your investment goals. Whether it be one property or one hundred, each goal requires a different lending approach.

Lawyer

Have you ever been sued? Those who have will tell you it's about as fun as squeezing lemon juice into a cut. This is where having a solid lawyer can save your ass. Legal contracts are a necessary evil when dealing in real estate. There's no way around it. Having a good real estate lawyer on your side can save you many hours of time down the road of wanting to smash your face into your desk. In addition to the usual legal paperwork involved in buying and selling a property, a good real estate lawyer can ensure you're well-protected on all your legal documents, from your leases and joint-venture agreements to how your corporation is structured.

Bookkeeper

Not enough good things can be said about an effective bookkeeper. One unfortunate symptom of real estate investing is paperwork. Like a shit-ton of paperwork. You've got your receipts, contracts, invoices, notices from the city, and the list goes on and on. When you have one or two properties, this bit is somewhat manageable, but as a portfolio grows, it feels as if the paperwork grows exponentially. Before long, it starts to feel as if all you're doing is organizing and documenting paperwork. You'll want nothing more than to throw it all into a trash can and set it on fire. If you like bookkeeping, more power to you, but if you'd rather spend that time on more important tasks such as raising money, growing your business, or spending time with friends and family, then a bookkeeper is indispensable. Not only will they do a better job than you but also won't create a place where hobos gather to keep warm. Totally worth it.

Accountant

When it comes to doing your taxes in your lifetime, there is a clear line between taxes before real estate investing and taxes after real estate investing. Doing taxes before real-estate investing is relatively simple, relatively inexpensive and feels like a speedbump in your otherwise cruisy life.

Doing taxes after real-estate investing is more akin to speeding down a mountain road where a wrong turn could send you over a cliff. Let's illustrate this point with a true story.

An investor, let's call him Tom, owned a condo he was renting out. After his mortgage, taxes, insurance, and condo fees, his cashflow was negative in that he had to pay into it every month in order to cover his expenses. It was not an ideal situation as an investor, but it happens.
That's fine. However, while doing his own taxes, he couldn't find a place on the tax software to put *condo fees*, so he just decided to leave it out. What this did, however, was made it look as if he was making money every month, whereas in reality, he was losing several hundred dollars every month because of the condo fees. This extra "income," in turn, boosted him into a higher tax bracket, so at the end of the year, he ended up owing thousands of dollars to the CRA. And this was on money he never actually made in the first place. Not only was this crappy investment eating his lunch every month, but he ended up with a double whammy of having to pay the CRA thousands of dollars for losing money.

The moral of the story is doing taxes with real estate investments can get complicated, so it may be better to spend the extra few hundred bucks, save yourself the hassle and the time and spend that irreplaceable currency on more valuable activities instead, like finding the next deal or spending time with your loved ones. Don't trip over dollars to get to the dimes.

Property Manager

Let's get one thing straight right now--no one is going to care about your properties as much as you will. That is a fact. If you want to grow your portfolio, however, a good property manager is vital to your success. You will get to a point where your management duties will eat into time better spent on high-value activities, so hiring a manager is inevitable if you plan to expand.

However, great time and care should be taken to ensure you find the right manager. Out of all your team members, you will likely be working with your property manager the most often, so it is important to ensure your values and management style are in line with each other.

Remember, to your tenants, the property managers are the faces of your company, so your reputation depends on who you hire.

Treat Your Investment as a Business

In addition to saving your sanity, your team allows you to treat your investing as a business (more on this in Chapter 11) by working *on* your business instead of *in* your business. Take your time building your team. Talk to other investors and see who they use. Ask for referrals. Don't rush it. If you end up hiring someone whom you find out later isn't the best fit, don't be afraid to let them go. This is your business, after all, and you have to do what's best for you. Real estate investing is a marathon, not a sprint, so long-term sustainability is key.

How I Built My Power Team

I'll be the first to admit building my power team was not cheap. I wasn't very good at asking for references and that was a hard-learned lesson. Don't make the same mistake I did. Some professionals charge a lot for their services, and more often than not, they're worth what you pay for, but as a new investor starting out, I didn't need anything particularly fancy and I had no money, so what I really needed was a good professional at a reasonable price.

I eventually got to know a few more investors in my real estate groups and asked them who they used for their services. Now I have a team on which I can rely to get the job done without breaking the bank.

Win-win for everyone!

You and your team may not be saving the world, but you are creating your own, and that's no small thing, so take your time to build a team you trust.

Next Actionable Step

Start putting together a list of professionals you want to be part of your real estate power team. The best way to do this is to get references from other real estate investors. You did go out and join a real estate investment group after the last chapter, right? You may have to go through a few references before you find those with whom you jive, so don't be discouraged if the first professionals you use don't work out.

CHAPTER 5

TENANT AND PROPERTY PROFILING

Meet Janet. Janet lives in Calgary, Alberta, Canada and has about $80,000 saved up. She wants to use that money to get into real estate investing. She's on the MLS for hours a day scouring neighborhoods, talking to Realtors and trying to find the best bang for her buck on an investment property. While she has $80,000, she doesn't want to blow it all in one go if she doesn't have to.

After looking at properties all over the city, she decides the area with the greatest returns is in the northeast quadrant of Calgary. That area has the best rent-to-price ratio in the whole city. She even finds an awesome deal--a 1200 square foot bungalow with a basement suite in the neighborhood of Dover for $290,000. Even with a 20% down payment, Janet only has to put down $58,000 and will still have $22,000 left over for any minor repairs.

Through rental sites, she finds she can rent her upstairs for around $1200 and her downstairs suite for $800. After the mortgage payments (30 year amortization at 3.69%), taxes and insurance, Janet is looking at over $600 a month in cashflow if she manages it herself. What an awesome deal. (We'll talk more about property analysis in Chapter 6.) She's practically shaking with excitement when she picks up the keys, just imagining the carefree future real estate will achieve for her.

Fast forward two years and Janet is about one phone call away from burning her investment property to the ground. In the last two years, she has already gone through five different tenants between her two suites and even had two midnight moves. What a nightmare those were. They didn't damage the property, but they'd left the place an absolute mess. Janet took a weekend cleaning up the first one, but after that ordeal, she'd ended up paying for a cleaning service the second time around.

Her current tenants have been there for a few months now, but not to say there aren't issues. Just last week, her basement tenant called to complain that the upstairs tenant looked at her funny as they crossed paths to their respective suites (This actually happened!). Janet was ready to put her head through a wall after that phone call.

Real estate prices have dipped in the last couple years, so Janet will take a loss if she were to sell her property now. She just has to tough it out for a bit longer until she can finally punt this thing to the next unsuspecting buyer. Her real *estate dream has turned into a recurring nightmare and she can't wait for it to end. Janet's really missing her old life...* Does this sound familiar?

We've heard more than our fair share of stories of problem tenants who don't pay rent but end up squatting for months, or tenants who leave a house completely trashed, leaving the owner with thousands of dollars of repairs.

Here's the good news--it doesn't have to be that way.

Tenant Profile

This is where everyone should start when looking for an investment property. Every investor should ask themselves, "What type of tenant do I want? What does my ideal tenant look like?"

The answer to that question will give you an idea what type of people you want to attract and to whom you want to market.

Now that you know what type of tenant you're looking for, the next question is, "What type of home would my ideal tenant like to live in?" For example, if you were to say your ideal tenant would be a young professional, a.k.a. a Millennial, then they would probably like to live in a modern apartment or a newer house with higher end furnishings such as stone countertops and stainless-steel appliances.

Another issue to factor in is *where* your ideal tenants would like to live. If we use the above example, they would most likely want to live close to downtown, where they can walk as much as possible if they're single, or if they're a young family, then in a nice neighborhood with parks and schools close by.

Developing your tenant profile is probably the most important thing an investor can do before deciding to buy an investment property, but unfortunately, it's also a step which a lot of new investors forget to take.

Tenant Avatar

No, this has nothing to do with The Last Airbender or giant blue humanoids on another planet. A tenant avatar is the description of your ideal prospect. If you could have just *one* tenant, then this would be the tenant you want. Having an avatar allows you to focus your marketing efforts, and more importantly, purchase the type of property in which they want to live.

Here are a few questions to ask when creating your tenant avatar:

1. How old are they?
2. What is their marital status?
3. Where do they want to live?
4. Any kids?
5. Do they have a pet?
6. How far did they go in school?
7. What is their job/how do they make a living?
8. What is their household income?
9. How long have they been working at their current job?
10. What are their personal goals?
11. What are their business goals?
12. What are their family goals?
13. What problem do they have and how can

you solve that problem?

The idea is to create a personality profile of your ideal tenant. With this in mind, you can build your whole investment strategy to catering to and attracting this particular tenant.

Let's try an example:

1. Age: 30-35 years old
2. Marital Status: Married less than five years
3. Wants to live in a nice newer home in a good neighborhood in close proximity to an elementary school
4. Children: Two kids
5. Pets: Small dog
6. Schooling: Both couples have post-secondary education
7. Work: relatively new to the work force but both have good professional jobs; both are corporate accountants
8. Household income: $150,000+ per year
9. Working at current jobs for five-to-seven years
10. Personal goals: pay off student loans, buy their own home
11. Business goals: establish their careers and climb up the corporate ladder; possibly start their own business
12. Family goals: raise their two kids well and not get divorced
13. Problem you can solve: Looking for a nice new home in a good neighborhood close to elementary schools where they can rent

while they save up to purchase their own home.

Based on all this information, create a short story about your avatar to better flesh out your idea. Don't be afraid to use names and get into the nitty gritty. An example of a story based on the above information might sound something like this:

Jake and Melissa both graduated from the University of Alberta four years ago with accounting degrees and were lucky enough to each get hired on by one of the Big Four out of an office in Calgary, Alberta. Jake got in with KPMG and Melissa got hired with Ernst and Young. Jake completed his CMA designation last year and is now focused on climbing the corporate ladder, while Melissa also got her CMA last year but is now working on her CFA (Certified Financial Analyst) to hopefully work for a hedge fund in a few years. They've been working hard and are almost finished paying off their combined $120,000 of student loans. Now that they've almost completed their first goal, they're looking forward to their next one--starting a family. As much as they love living in their two- bedroom high rise apartment in downtown Calgary, which is within walking distance of their favorite coffee shops and restaurants, they're going to need more room. Besides, their building doesn't allow pets and they want to get a dog next year.

Being busy paying off their student loans, they haven't had a chance to save up for a down payment for a place of their own, so they're going to have to rent for now.
Scouring Rentfaster and Kijiji, they come across a house for rent in the neighborhood of Tuscany in the west of Calgary. It is $2,100 a month for a 2000 square foot home with an attached front garage and an unfinished basement. "Not bad

at all," thinks Melissa. It's more than the $1,800 they're paying now for their downtown condo, but they'll have a ton more room and a yard for their future dog and kids. There's even an elementary and junior-high school in the area.

With each of them making over $80,000 a year, they can easily afford the rent and still have enough left over to save up for a place of their own in a couple of years. In the meantime, they can take their dog and young one to the park and not worry about them finding a used needle or being run over by downtown traffic. Perfect.

Reading that story, you'd almost think Jake and Melissa are real people, and that's exactly what you want to do. You want them to be so real to you that you can understand their wants, needs and frustrations, and then you solve their problems by providing them exactly what they're looking for.

Once you know *who* you're looking for and *in what* and *where* they'd like to live, then it really helps to narrow down the areas in a city in which for you to buy. By focusing on a smaller area, you can really dig into the pricing of the area and you will more easily be able to recognize what is considered a good deal and jump on it right away.

Don't Just Look at Price

A mistake many investors make is to buy solely based on price. The upside of this strategy is the *return-on-investment* (ROI) often looks amazing. A cheap house with good rents = great returns. However, there are a lot of qualitative factors such an investor wouldn't consider, and those could very well be the things which makes an investor want to give up and throw in the towel.

The bottom line is, *don't* buy an investment property based only on the price you pay. If you find a place which costs more but is in a better neighborhood, is a newer home (less maintenance issues), attracts better tenants and still generates cashflow, then that's a much better choice in the long run. More than likely, it will generate a lower return *on paper*, but in reality, you're spending less time, money and effort to manage it. So, in the long run, you have to ask yourself what your sanity and emotional well-being is worth.

How I Found My Niche

When I first started, I nearly fell into the price trap too. I had already bought one property at that point--a single, detached home in Edmonton, in a new neighborhood that was a new build. I had some solid, freshly graduated engineers renting from me at that point so everything was good. I wanted to buy my next home, but I was pretty strapped for cash, so I started looking in more affordable areas of Edmonton. By affordable, I mean questionable. Great places if you're looking for a bar fight or to get caught up in a drug deal while going for a walk at night.

However, property prices were cheap. We're talking low-to-mid $200's for a detached home, compared to the $400+ paid for my first property, so it looked very attractive from a numbers perspective. I hadn't really thought about tenant profiles at that point, but thankfully my dad and a couple of investors I'd chatted with convinced me places like those were more trouble than they were worth. In retrospect, I am infinitely grateful and have them to thank for coming this far in my investing career. If I *had* bought one of those properties, and knowing my personal bullshit limit, I would've thrown in the towel a long time ago.

Things really clicked when I bought my second property close to my first – with joint-venture partners this time and witnessed for myself how the property you have attracts the tenants for whom you're looking. Due to a higher mortgage, we naturally had to price our rent pretty high to make sure the cashflow worked, but as a result of higher rents, it automatically filtered out any low-income tenants. And since this was a new property, it attracted individuals and young families who had good incomes and preferred a newer product--in other words, mostly young professionals. I've been focused on this type of investment property ever since. Other perks which come with this strategy are very low maintenance costs, as everything is new, and very little tenant management, as the tenants are typically less needy. The one downside is higher up-front costs, but in my opinion, this is totally worth it. Not to say this strategy is for everyone, but if you're like me (lazy with a low bullshit limit) then I'd strongly suggest you look into it.

Next Actionable Step

Your next step is to think about what type of tenant profile you'd ideally prefer and create a tenant avatar for that ideal tenant. Use the questions earlier in the chapter to guide you. There's no such thing as too much detail. The better you understand your tenant, the better you can provide them what they want. Do this *before* you decide what type of property in which you ultimately want to invest.

CHAPTER 6

PROPERTY ANALYSIS

Yay! Math time!

Some people love it, some hate it, and it's definitely not the most exciting part of the business, but it's arguably the most important step, so let's dig in. Property analysis is kind of like getting a prostate exam--it's not pleasant, but it has to be done. Otherwise, it could lead to a cancer metastasizing and ruining the rest of your life.

Before you start looking at the numbers for a property, there are a few questions you should first consider:

1. Is the GDP (Gross Domestic Product) of the area going up or down?
2. Are there jobs in the area?
3. Who are the main employers?

4. Is there net population growth or loss?

Let's look at each of these in more detail.

GDP Growth

How the economy is doing should be the first thing you consider when you're looking at where to invest. If the economy is improving, then obviously, that's a good thing. An improving economy means more jobs, more people moving in to fill said jobs and more rental demand, which eventually leads to higher rents and higher real-estate prices. That's a good time to be a real-estate investor and kind of sounds like a no-brainer.
But what about if the economy is circling the drain, so to speak? If that's the case, then opposite events may be happening. If there are no jobs, people are moving away to find jobs elsewhere, there are more vacancies and lower rents, then this could all lead to lower real estate prices.

The next question you should ask is: Is this a cyclical economy? If the answer is *no* then you should get the hell out of there and look somewhere else. If it's *yes* and you know the economy will bounce back, such as in Alberta with oil, for example, then this might be an opportunity in disguise. Homeowners may be tight on cash and more desperate to sell, which leads to more willingness to negotiate and lower prices. Many potential buyers may also be in dire financial straits, so you'll have less competition. If you're in a position to get into the market, this may be a great time. So, look at economic reports from banks and economists and take action accordingly.

Job Prospects

Is employment increasing or decreasing in the area at which you're looking? As mentioned above, an increase in jobs means more people moving into the area who need accommodations and increases rental demand. If unemployment is increasing, then the opposite is true. Banks and economists typically release monthly reports where you can find this information. You also want to compare these numbers to the national average to know whether you're ahead or behind the curve. Being ahead is better.

Major Employers in the Area

Major employers are defined as companies that employ more than 100 full-time individuals on a regular basis. The more major employers in an area, the more stable the job market, and in turn, the more stable the working population. If there are only two or three major employers in an area, you're going to be in big trouble if one of them decides to leave or go out of business. Ideally, you want a town with a good number of major employers, so the economy is more resilient in the event of a downturn. In comparing Edmonton and Calgary, for example, Edmonton held up better during the oil recession of 2015-2017. The majority of the oil company's head offices resided in Calgary, so when the recession hit and people got laid off, the vacancies in Calgary skyrocketed and rents went down faster than the Oilers' chances of making the playoffs this year. Edmonton, on the other hand, had a more diversified economy, with a large number of government jobs, as well as manufacturing and construction, in addition to oilfield-related work. By comparison, Edmonton rents and vacancies still went down, but not as sharply as Calgary's.

Population Growth

If nothing else, the population growth or decline in an area is a pretty good sign of whether the economy is doing well. People won't move to a place if there are no jobs, so population growth is a good thing. If you find that the population is decreasing, you should consider looking elsewhere. This information is typically listed on the city's website. Again, see if the area's population growth is higher than the national average.

Once you find a city or town where the economy is growing, there are more job opportunities with a number of major employers and the population is growing, it's time to look at how to analyze the numbers of an actual property.

Property Analysis

The main point of property analysis, or for any business for that matter, is to make sure the money you make is more than the money it costs to operate the asset. Sounds pretty simple, right?

Let's start with the easy part – *income*. For a *buy-and-hold* investment property, that's the rent. When you're looking at the rent, include all sources of income you derive from the property, including any parking spots, garages or storage spaces you rent out in addition to the main living areas.

Researching Rents

In order to price your units accordingly, there are a few ways to find out what current rents are in an area. You can hire a company to do an official rental analysis of the area, which will give you an official report. This type of analysis is usually only requested by banks when you're applying for financing on a vacant rental property. Otherwise, there are other ways to do your own research for free.

The first thing you should do is Google *house rentals in your area* and discover which main sites pop up. These are likely the sites most people go to find rentals in your area, so you should start with those sites. Find rental rates for similar properties in your area and start from there. Padmapper.com is a good site, as well. They aggregate all the listings from various sites and list them all on one site. Some popular rental sites include Rentfaster.ca, Rentboard.ca, Kijiji.com, Facebook Marketplace and Craigslist. In addition, these sites are also great places to post your rental when it comes time to do that.

Expenses

As for expenses, there are a few more to consider. They can include the following:

- Mortgage payments
- Property Taxes
- Property Insurance
- Utilities
- Strata/condo Fees
- Property Management
- Vacancies
- Maintenance Costs

Property management, vacancies, and maintenance costs may not be monthly recurring costs (sometimes known as *soft costs*), especially if you are managing the property yourself.

However, they are still inevitable costs which have to be accounted for and are often overlooked by many new investors.

Property Management

In Canada, for single family homes, most property managers charge around 10% of the gross rent per month as their fee. They also charge a markup on the contractors they have to hire for any maintenance issues and charge additionally to fill or renew a tenant. In the end, you'll be paying close to 14% a month. Unless you want to manage the properties for the rest of your life however, they are a necessary part of your team, especially if you're growing your portfolio.

Vacancies

You should account for a one-month vacancy a year for your rentals. This comes out to 8% of your gross rent per month (1/12 x 100 = 8%). You may not have a vacancy in a particular year, and that's great, but you want to account for it so that you're not caught off-guard with unexpected expenses when you do.

Maintenance Costs

Maintenance costs depends a lot on the age of the property, but even with a brand-new property, there are still maintenance costs. Typically, for an older property (10 years or more), you want to set aside about 5% a month, whereas you can probably get away with 3% on a newer property. There are no hard-and fast-rules, and there will always be unexpected expenses, but at least you're prepared--and that's what counts.

Cash Flow

Now that we've accounted for all the income and expenses, it's time to calculate cashflow. A typical cashflow calculation looks something like this:

Monthly Rental Income	$2,000
Monthly Garage Rental Income	$200
Total Monthly Rental Income	**$2,200**
Monthly Mortgage &Interest Payments	$1,300
Monthly Property Taxes	$200
Monthly Property Insurance	$100
Utilities*	$300
Strata/Condo Fees	None
Property Management @ 10%	$220
Vacancy @ 8%	$160
Maintenance @ 3%	$60
Total Monthly Rental Expenses	**$2,040**
Total Monthly Income	$2,200
Total Monthly Expenses	-$2,040
TOTAL MONTHLY CASHFLOW	**$160**

* Paid by Tenant

At first glance, $160 may not seem like much, but think about it this way. You've just factored in all possible costs, including some you might not even incur, and you're *still* making money. Factor back in the vacancy and maintenance costs and you're up to $380 a month. If you're
managing it yourself for now, then you're up to $600 a month! Don't forget you're still paying down the mortgage by about $600-$700 a month as well. $160 in cashflow

doesn't look so bad anymore, huh?

But just because the property isn't costing as much as you think doesn't mean you get to spend the extra, which leads us to our next very important topic.

Reserve Fund

Every investment property should have a reserve fund, a.k.a. sleep-at-night fund, a.k.a. not- having-to-explain-to-your-spouse-why-you-took-money-out-of-junior's-college-fund fund.

Remember all those extra expenses you accounted for in your analysis but didn't have to pay? This is where that goes. You want to start the account with enough to cover at least one mortgage payment and during the following months, build it up to ideally have enough to cover you for three months. This should be enough for you not to worry about filling a vacancy right away and gives you some time to find a good tenant. It should also be enough to cover any maintenance expenses which might pop up along the way. Knowing you have enough set aside to handle any unexpected expenses which may come up is more important than you know for your mental health, so it cannot be emphasized enough how important having a reserve fund is.

SET UP A RESERVE FUND!

Gross and Total Debt Service Ratios

This is how you'll figure out whether the banks will even loan you the money in the first place. When lenders look at affordability, they typically look at two things--the Gross Debt Service (GDS) ratio and the Total Debt Service (TDS) ratio. The GDS ratio is the percentage of your gross income needed to pay for your monthly housing costs including the principal, interest, taxes and heat. You'll also need to include 50% of your strata/condo fees if you have any. The industry standard is typically 35% so lenders like to see your GDS below this before they qualify you for a mortgage.

(Principal + Interest + Taxes + Heat) / Gross Monthly Income x 100 = GDS (<35%)

The TDS ratio is the GDS ratio *plus* any additional monthly debts you may have, as well. For example, if you have a $500 monthly car payment, $100 interest payment on a line of credit, and $1000 of alimony, then those get factored in. The industry standard lenders don't like to see a borrower exceed on their TDS is 42%.

(GDS + All Monthly Debt Obligations) / Gross Monthly Income x 100 = TDS (<42%) Let's look at an example:
Dylan has a gross income of $5000 a month. He wants to buy a $450,000 home where the monthly mortgage payment is estimated to be about $1620. The taxes are $280, and heat is $80 a month. He also has a $450 monthly car payment and puts $100 a month towards paying off his credit card.

GDS: ($1620 + $280 + $80) / $5000 = 0.396 x 100 = 39.6%

TDS: ($1620 + $280 + $80 + $450 + $100) / $5000 = 0.518 x 100 = 51.8%

Based on these numbers, Dylan's GDS and TDS both exceed the industry standard lenders like to see and he would have a hard time qualifying for a mortgage. His options at this point are to opt for a less expensive house, cut his expenses, earn more money or all the above.

These ratios are industry guidelines and not set in stone, so some lenders are more flexible than others. If you exceed these ratios by a wide margin however, there's a good chance you'll run into some difficulties getting qualified.

Cashflow: How Much is Enough?

When I started investing and learning how to analyze properties, one question kept popping into my head--how much cashflow is enough for an investment to be considered a good investment? I've taken courses and questioned numerous investors but could never get a consistent answer. Some courses tell you to not invest in anything that cashflows less than 8%. For simplicity sake, if a house cost $100,000, then your yearly rent should be $8,000 or more (8,000/100,000 x 100 = 8%). I found this number works for some properties in... shall we say less desirable neighborhoods where I initially wanted to invest. If you live in an area where this number works and the properties are in good shape, go for it. It's a solid metric and a great way to define a good investment.

For myself, I needed something less stringent. After talking to a number of successful real- estate investors, I decided on the *$150 rule*. It's pretty simple. After all expenses, including management, vacancy and maintenance, if the property still cashflows at least $150, then it's a good buy. The $150 allows for any increase in interest rates and adding in the soft costs allow for a pretty decent amount to go into the reserve fund every month. It's also a low enough number that you won't pass on too many good deals compared to a stricter parameter. If you are in a similar situation, you might want to consider adopting the *$150 rule*, as well.

Debt Coverage Ratio (DCR)

Another metric to consider in addition to the *$150 Rule* is The Debt Coverage Ratio or DCR. The DCR is the ratio of rental income vs expenses for a property. For example, if the cost of the mortgage, taxes and insurance is $1000 and the rental income is $1200 then the DCR is $1200/$1000 = 1.2.

Now why do we need to know this and how is it important? First, the higher the DCR the better because that means more cash flow for you. Secondly, and more importantly, the banks look at those numbers when you want to expand your portfolio. When you want to buy more than one rental property, the banks will look at your current portfolio and calculate the DCR. If your DCR is greater than 1.2 — as in, your rent is 20% more than your expenses — then a lot of times, the banks will consider your debt a wash and won't factor in that cost when they calculate your Gross and Total Debt Service ratios.

Now, what can you do with this information? If you're planning on building a real estate portfolio over the long term, it's a good idea to start off with a solid foundation. Start with buying properties with a DCR of at least 1.2, if not better. If it's below 1.2, some banks will factor in the *whole* debt into your Debt Service calculation, not just the difference between 1.2 and whatever you may have. Banks will find a way to try to cap you eventually, but it's your job to figure out ways around it. By keeping to this rule, you can keep growing your portfolio until that happens.

One upside if you already have the *$150 Rule* down is the banks don't look at your soft costs when they calculate your DCR. So, your management fees as well as your maintenance and vacancy allowances you accounted for in your calculations above can be added back into your cash flow to determine what the banks would get if they were to calculate your DCR. If you satisfy the ***$150 Rule***, there's a good chance you satisfy the DCR as well, but always do your due diligence.

Analysis Paralysis

A lot of new investors get stuck at this stage. They analyze a million properties, but they never pull the trigger to buy their first. It's understandable to be scared and there are plenty of reasons to be scared, as there are a lot of risks in real estate investing. There are, however, ways to mitigate those risks, as we'll discuss in Chapter 11.

One of the reasons people get anxious about investing in real estate is because they fear not knowing what to do if a situation they've never encountered arises. This applies to every situation in your life and not just in real estate. For example, say you chartered a personal plane somewhere, just you and the pilot. Before getting on the plane, the pilot warns you that he has narcolepsy and if he passes out, you're going to have to take over piloting until he wakes up. If you've never piloted a plane before, there's no way in hell you're getting on that plane.

However, if you have a pilot's license and have flown that model of plane before, you're much more inclined to jump on that ride. I'm not saying it's a good idea, but you'd likely be less anxious if you knew what to do.

The purpose of this book is to give you enough tools so you feel comfortable enough to pull the trigger and not lose your shit when a problem comes up because you have an idea what to do, or at least know where to find the answer. You're never going to know everything, and that's all right, because no one does. But that's where ongoing education comes in. If you're hoping to figure out every step of the way before you take your first step, then you're never going to get anywhere.

With *buy-and-hold* investing, it's the time *in* the market that counts, so the sooner you can get a property under your belt, the sooner you can start building wealth.

Next Actionable Step

The only way to get better at analyzing properties is by doing. So, go on the MLS, find a property you may want to purchase and perform an analysis on it to see how well it cashflows. The more you do it, the more comfortable you'll become, and soon you'll be able to look at a property and know right off the bat whether it'll be a good or bad deal from all the deals you've analyzed.

Analyze one deal before the end of the day. Go now!

CHAPTER 7

FINDING YOUR FIRST INVESTMENT

Anyone who's ever gone ocean fishing will tell you that you almost always need to hire a fishing guide if it's not something you do for a living. They have all the equipment, they know where all the best fish are hiding, and they know what they're doing so you don't become another statistic. The ocean is a big and dangerous place. Trying to find a lost ship out there is like trying to find a needle in a haystack. You pay a lot for the captain's experience and expertise, but you generally enjoy a pleasant time highlighted by some exciting moments, rather than a re- enactment of Tom Hanks in Castaway.

The same goes when you're looking for your first property. You generally want a good Realtor on your side, who knows the lay of the land and who can tell you the good areas from the bad and where the good deals are. I highlighted the benefits of having a good Realtor on your team, so I'm not going to beat a dead horse, but hiring a Realtor, especially one who's worked with investors, should be a serious consideration, especially if you're unfamiliar with the area.

There are other tactics to find a property, but I would only recommend these if you're familiar with the area and are confident in what you're looking for. These may include looking for listings on Kijiji or Craigslist, knocking on doors and soliciting the owners to sell. You might try direct mail, where you send out letters soliciting owners to sell, or you can talk to builders directly to see what they have to offer. The benefit of these methods is the seller doesn't have to pay any Realtor fees, so you may have more negotiating room. The downside is it's a lot of work. You're essentially trading money for time, so choose what works best for your lifestyle.

How I Find My Properties

As I've iterated before, my goal with my real estate investments is to do as little as possible while still owning the asset. As a result, I only like new properties. I typically negotiate a deal with a builder to construct a purpose-built rental with a legal secondary suite and separate utilities. The latter is nice, as it is one less thing I'll have to deal with down the road. The benefit of going through a builder is I get exactly what I want, it's brand new so maintenance costs are negligible the first several years, it's covered under warranty, tenants *love* a new product and I don't have to worry about a bidding war. I make it sound like the best strategy ever, but there are downsides, including a typically higher down payment, the cost to landscape and fence the property and very little room to add value through your own renovations. Remember--this is my strategy targeting *my* ideal tenant profile. Yours may be different, so adjust your strategy accordingly.

Next Actionable Step

If you're at the stage where you're ready to start looking to buy an investment property, reach out to another investor for a recommendation for a good Realtor and meet for coffee to see how they can help you and if they're a good fit. If you're brave, you can start knocking on doors and ask if the owners are interested in selling. The worse that will happen is they'll tell you they're not interested and for you to get lost. In the best-case scenario, you'll get a great deal. If it goes poorly, you're never going to see them again anyway, so what do you have to lose?

Make some calls or pound the pavement but make something happen.

CHAPTER 8

PURCHASE AND NEGOTIATION

Amber is a real estate investor who's gotten herself into a predicament. She went into a house investment with a joint venture partner using mostly the joint venture money. Wanting to show she had skin in the game, Amber put down $10,000, while the JV partner put down $100,000 to purchase a high-end, up-down, legally suited house. Unbeknownst to Amber however, was that her JV partner had borrowed their $100,000 from a line of credit and did not factor in how much it would cost to service the interest payments. You can probably see where this is going.

The JV partner had a lot of home equity but was house poor and therefore couldn't service the debt on his own and had to take money from the cashflow of the house to supplement in order to keep from going into even more debt. The JV agreement was that Amber would manage the property, and the cashflow and equity would be split fifty-fifty. Half of the cash being withdrawn by her partner belonged to her, but she felt she couldn't tell him to stop as it would have gotten them into even more debt than they already were.

What was Amber to do? What would you do?

Believe it or not, this situation dragged on for two years before the JV partner finally offered to buy Amber out. The JV figured that if he had full control of the property, then he could eventually sell it and recoup some of his money. The property had built up around $20,000 in equity and cashflow by that point, so Amber's share was $10,000 plus her initial deposit of $10,000, making her total buyout $20,000. If Amber really wanted to push it, she could have asked her partner for an additional share for managing the property over the past two years, as well, but she decided it was better to get out of the property, let the JV figure out his financial issues on his own and not ruin a good friendship. Oh, and one last thing--the partner didn't have enough to pay Amber right away.

In the end, they came to an agreement where the JV would pay Amber $10,000 now and pay the other $10,000 over the next two years in $2,500 installments every six months interest free.

Do you agree with what Amber did? What would you have done differently?

There are a couple of lessons to be learned from this story. One is to always make sure your JV partner doesn't fall into dire financial straits because of the investment. Ensure they've done the math and can afford any and all payments they might incur from purchasing the investment. You don't have to do the math for them but be certain they've done the math for themselves. You may not think it's your problem, but when your JV partner starts taking money out of your joint account to pay *their* debts or goes into bankruptcy when their name is on the mortgage, you can bet your ass it's also going to be your problem.

The second lesson is to make every negotiation a win-win as much as possible. A good example is Amber's story. She got paid what she was due from the investment, removed herself from a financially messy situation and her JV got control of the house to have a better chance of digging himself out of debt. Everybody wins!

Just because you can screw someone over doesn't mean you should. Aside from the benefit of not being an asshole, the other party will remember your graciousness and might become a valuable contact in the future. Why make enemies when you can make friends, right?

Knowing What You Want

Before you jump into any formal negotiations, be sure to do your homework on the property you want. Be clear on the age, the style (i.e. townhouse, bungalow or two-story), the size of the house, the zoning--to make sure you can build a secondary suite if that's your plan, any renovations you'll need to make, your budget for said renovations and the finishing, if it's a new build.

When it comes to price, make sure you have comparables of recent sales, so you know whether you're getting a good deal or are getting ripped off. ALWAYS have a maximum price you're willing to pay. This price is based three things:

1. Market Comps - you should never pay over market
2. Your Budget - what you can afford with the resources you have
3. Cashflow Analysis - the property has to have positive cashflow at the price you pay

Lastly, be ready with your BATNA (Best Alternative to a Negotiated Agreement). A BATNA is like your backup plan. If negotiations fail, you turn to your BATNA as your Plan B. This may mean you go with a different property or a different builder, and very often it simply means you walk away. If the math doesn't work or the property is not a good fit for your portfolio, then walking away may be your only alternative. It's not worth it to overpay for a property or have it keep you up at night. There will always be other deals. Besides, walking away is a great negotiation tactic, which may be enough to get the seller to agree to your terms.

Always have a BATNA.

Pressure Points

Try to figure out your opponent's pain points. Ask them questions, creep on their social media and talk to their neighbors. The goal is to figure out what they most need, where they're having the greatest issues and then to exploit those areas of weakness. The goal is still to aim for a win-win scenario, so I'm not saying you should shove in a knife and twist. Rather, find out what you can do to help them and in turn, they may be more agreeable to your terms. For example, the sellers may need the house sold in a week. Otherwise, they're going to be carrying two mortgages. You can make that happen, but they have to lower their price.

Everyone typically has a pain point, and if you can find out what that is and help them relieve the pain, they will often be more than happy to do whatever you ask.

Financing and Conditions

When you submit an offer, your Realtor will ask what conditions you want attached to the offer. The deal is subject to the successful completion of these conditions when an offer is accepted. If they are not met within a specific time frame, then the deal is off. Conditions you may see include *financing, inspection* and in some provinces, an *RPR (Real Property Report)*. Let's go over these in a bit more detail.

Financing

The financing condition means when your offer is accepted, the banks have to approve of you getting the mortgage before the deal goes through. There are a lot of incidences where an offer is accepted and then the buyer finds out for one reason or another they're not approved for financing on the property. This is a shitty position to be in, but fortunately, this can be easily avoided. *Before* you go house shopping, reach out to your mortgage broker and ask them to do a preapproval for you. This tells you how much the banks will lend you and how much house you can actually afford. This has the added benefit of narrowing your search criteria and saving yourself and your Realtor a ton of time. This is also one condition you can waive to make yourself look more attractive to the sellers if you already have a preapproval.

Interestingly, as mentioned in the DCR section earlier, if you already have a rental property, as long as the monthly rent exceeds the cost of owning the property by 20% or more, some banks don't factor that mortgage amount into your debt-to-income calculations. For example, you own a property and for simple math's sake, it costs $1,000 for you to service the mortgage, property taxes, property insurance and maintenance. If you can rent it for $1,200 or more (200/1,000 = 0.2 x 100 = 20%), then the banks will look at you as if that debt doesn't exist.

Pretty cool, right? This is why you always need to make sure your properties cashflow. It makes it very hard to grow your portfolio when banks aren't willing to lend you money.

Inspection

This is probably the most important of all the conditions, and with the exception of some very specific scenarios, I would never recommend waiving this condition. Ensure the condition reads, "This agreement is conditional upon the inspection of the property by a home inspector of the purchaser's choice and expense, and receipt of a report satisfactory to him in his sole and absolute discretion." This condition basically says if the inspection is not to the buyer's satisfaction, they have the right to walk away at their sole and absolute discretion. This last bit is important, so don't forget to add it.

A good home inspector will crawl on the roof, poke around in the attic and peek in every nook and cranny to note any problems a homeowner may have to worry about, such as leaks, inefficient insulation, cracks in the foundation, replacement of any major items like the furnace, hot-water tank or roof and the list goes on. A home inspection typically costs $500-$700, which may seem like a lot of money to spend for a house you might not even buy but think of it as an insurance policy. You're about to make a purchase that costs *hundreds of thousands of dollars*. If $500 can catch a problem where walking away from the deal will save you tens of thousands of dollars, then the inspector was worth every nickel.

Note: for older houses (pre-1980s), you may want to pay extra (typically $300) to do a scope of the main sewer line to see if there is any damage or collapse of the line for the portion that belongs to the property. If there's a collapse in the line, sewage could eventually back up into the house. And if that wasn't bad enough, if the collapse is on your property, it's your responsibility to fix it and it's not cheap. The pipe has to be excavated and replaced, so you're looking at a $5,000 to $20,000 job. If the damage is on the city side however, then they will cover the cost, which could make or break a deal. So, a scope is definitely worth considering for older properties.

RPR (Real Property Report)

An RPR condition on a purchase contract is not standard across Canada. For example, in Ontario, they rarely ask for the RPR, but it's a standard condition on the purchase contracts in Alberta. An RPR is a legal document of a property prepared by provincial land surveyors which shows the property, boundaries, and any structures present so the buyers know what they should be getting. An RPR contains:

- Legal description and municipal address of the property
- Date of land title search and date RPR was done
- Certificate of Title (land title) number and names of registered owner(s)

- Location and description of all buildings and structures (e.g. decks, fences) with dimensions, directions, and distances from the property boundaries
- Location and dimensions of any visible encroachments (i.e. buildings or structures which are too close or even beyond the property line)
- Designation of adjacent properties, roads, lanes
- Evidence of municipal compliance (i.e. the RPR has been reviewed by your municipality and adheres to all municipal bylaws and regulations. They usually stamp and date compliance directly on the RPR)

- Illustrations of any easements that affect the property (an easement is an agreement between the property owner and some other party, usually your municipal authority or utility, for them to utilize part of your property as needed)
- Certified Land Surveyor's duly signed certification and opinion on any concerns
- Copyright of the RPR to the land survey company

The purpose of getting an RPR when you're buying is to make sure that the structures on the property are actually on the RPR as well, because if they aren't, the sellers never got a permit for that structure and it could cost you a lot of money to correct that deficiency.

Note: You can get the seller to buy title insurance if they don't have an RPR and don't want to pay to have one done. Title insurance can cover the buyer in the event there is an *unknown* deficiency on the property. But I would first consult your lawyer before taking this step, so it doesn't bite you in the ass down the road when you find out things are not covered after all.

My Experience with Purchase and Negotiations

I was born in Canada, so I'll be the first to admit I am not the best at negotiations. Bartering and negotiating just isn't a big part of North American life or culture. We go to a store, see a price on the price tag and pay the price listed without thinking twice. We go to the grocery store and apples are $1.99/lb, so we pay $1.99/lb with no questions asked. The only times we really negotiate are on the big-ticket items in our lives like cars or homes. But how often does that really happen? Most people can count those moments with one hand. It's not something we're used to doing, and if you don't do if often, you probably don't do it well.

My parents are full-on Asian. They were born in Vietnam, grew up there and moved to Canada when they were adults, so haggling and negotiating was just a way of life for them. The thought process over there is *everything is negotiable,* and you never pay full price on anything. The vendors expect haggling, as well, so everything is marked up with room to negotiate. A lot of what I've learned about negotiating, I've learned from watching my parents and reading books like **Getting to Yes** and **Never Split the Difference**. It's a vital skill when doing business, and it's not something taught in school, so it's important to do some self-learning in this field.

When I get into talks to buy a house, I make sure all my analysis is done so I know what my maximum price is going to be in order to generate the amount of cashflow I need. I have a list of all the things I want for my house, like the level of finishing, separate utilities if doing a new build, a deck, etc. I do the majority of my negotiations with builders, so I always let them set the price before negotiating that down. I often don't disclose my maximum price at the beginning, and as a rule of thumb, you should never be the first one to state your price. You never know what the other party is thinking. They could have set a lower price than you expect.

In one of my last negotiations, I was in talks with a buyer to sell one of my properties. The asking price was $350,000, while the bank appraised the property at $335,000. The purchase contract had already been signed and accepted by me, but there was the question of the $15,000 difference in financing that the bank wouldn't cover. I had a few options:

1. Sell at the lower appraised value and accept the loss of $15,000.
2. Split the difference, so I would accept a loss of $7,500 and the buyer would put forward the same amount.
3. Ask the buyer to put up the $15,000 difference or otherwise not sell the house.

I really didn't want to lose the $15,000, but I wasn't sure what the buyer was willing to pay. When we met for talks, I was ready to offer to split the difference, but as I opened my mouth to make the offer, I caught myself and simply asked, "What are your thoughts on this deal?" To my complete surprise, the buyers *really* wanted the house, so they offered to pay the $15,000 difference out of their own pockets. If I had been the first to make my offer, I would've left $7,500 on the table! That was a fist-pump moment for sure. Again, don't be the first to make an offer.

As a real estate investor, we have a few useful negotiation

tactics which aren't available to the average home buyer. Here's a few you can try:

1. There's more where this came from. We're investors, so we typically don't stop at one property. If talking with the seller's agent, make this fact known and see if they can get their client to sell at a lower price. You can hint at doing more business with this agent in the future. The same goes with a builder--get you a good deal and you'll consider buying more in the future or will refer other investors to the builder.
2. Buy in bulk. If you get a good deal and you have the funds, consider buying more than one house from the builder to further push down the price. If you alone don't have the funds, get other investors in on the same deal to negotiate a discount.
3. Patience. As an investor, we can afford to wait. If the seller price is unreasonably high, a few extra weeks on the market may change their mind.
4. Walk away. This one is the best card we have up our sleeve. As an investor, we don't HAVE to buy a house. If the seller isn't willing to negotiate or meet the price you desire, just walk away. If the sellers are motivated, this move can do wonders.

Set your criteria, do your due diligence, find their pain points and don't be afraid to walk away. If you fail, just try again. It's all part of the game.

Next Actionable Step

Call up your cell phone provider and negotiate a better deal for your plan. If you're not used to negotiating, this is a perfect place to start. You have *ZERO* downside. If you negotiate a better deal, that's a win for you. If they say no, you're no worse off than you are now. The point is to get you comfortable with the negotiating process without any of the risk. You can't lose here, so get to it!

CHAPTER 9

MARKETING FOR TENANTS

Finding the right tenant is what makes or breaks most first-time real estate investors. A terrible tenant will ruin your life, whereas a great tenant will make you wonder why you didn't invest in real estate sooner. The former type will be late on rent, complain to you about every little thing, start a grow-op and essentially try to turn your rental into their own version of Yoda's swamp hut on Dagobah. The latter type of tenant will pay rent on time every month and you won't hear from them until they're ready to move out, which is when you'll find out they've repainted the whole house for you and made the place cleaner than when they moved in.

Which tenant would you want--the former or the latter? Hint: the answer rhymes with batter.

If you've already created a tenant avatar and bought a property that suits that avatar, then you're already halfway there. The next step is to *attract* that tenant. This isn't as hard as you think. There are really only three steps--pricing the rent appropriately, writing a good ad and good visuals. Let's go through each of these in detail.

Pricing the Rent Right

Do an internet search on "homes for rent in <u>your city here</u>" and Google will show you the most popular sites on which people look for rental properties where you live. That's where you'll want to start your research. Rentfaster.ca, Facebook Marketplace and Padmapper.com are good resources for this. Specify the type of property (e.g. condo, duplex, townhouse, detached, etc.), the number of bedrooms and bathrooms and search. The map view is useful, as it allows you to focus on the area of the city closest to your rental and lets you see what others are charging in the area. Other things to keep in mind when looking at comparable rentals are the size of the property and the quality of the interior finishings. For comparables, you want to find properties which resemble yours as closely as possible. On the other hand, if all you find are older places with lower quality finishings (e.g. carpet versus hardwood, laminate versus stone countertops), then you can charge more if yours is a newer, shinier product. People (especially Millennials) nearly always prefer a newer, shinier product and are willing to pay for that quality, so don't be afraid to charge a bit more. You can always lower the rent after a week or two if you don't get any immediate interest.

An alternative to researching your own rents is to hire a rental research company to do a rental analysis study for you, but these are pricey and often unnecessary. Banks sometimes require an official report from these companies to qualify a rental purchase for financing, but if you don't need one, there are enough resources out there now for you to do your own research with similar results.

Writing a Good Advertisement

Writing a winning ad is important. You want to be able to tell a good story and make the reader imagine themselves as part of that story. You want to evoke an emotional response. The more compelling the ad, the stronger the response. Many of the ads you see just list the features of the property like a shopping list, but when was the last time you got excited about a shopping list? For a good ad, you want to list the *benefits* of the features, not just the features themselves. Here's an example of a good rental ad:

Welcome to your gorgeous new home at 1517 170th Ave NW in Northeast Edmonton! You will love this beautiful, custom-built two-story home of your dreams. Seriously, this place will blow you away.

Located in the quiet neighborhood of Fraser, this 2,500 square foot luxury dream home is a sight to behold. The contemporary architectural detail will awe your friends and wow your neighbors. Enter the main doors and be taken away by the open space and natural light pouring in from every angle.

Continuing through the main floor, you will notice the spacious den with a stylish sliding barn door before moving onto the beautiful gourmet kitchen complete with quartz countertops, stainless-steel appliances, soft-closing cabinets and a generous walk-through pantry. Chat and relax with a couple of friends at the eating bar or cook up a storm and serve your guests in the brightly-lit dining area. Afterward, you can sit back and relax in the adjacent living area in this wonderful open-concept design.

From the kitchen, walk through the pantry and the well-appointed mud room with built-in storage lockers to the oversized, double-attached garage with enough room to house a heavy- duty pickup with room to spare.

Heading upstairs, you'll find a bright, spacious bonus room with a wet bar in the corner--another great space in which to entertain guests or kick back after a long day at work. Down the hall, you'll encounter two spacious bedrooms before arriving at the Master Suite, which includes a positively massive walk-in closet and an ensuite that will make your jaw drop.

Put it all together and you have a home you have to see to believe. This house is newly-built and never lived in, so be the first to experience this modern wonder for yourself.

With the Anthony Henday just around the corner and the Manning Crossing shopping center just five minutes down the street, access and convenience couldn't be easier.

Give us a call and set up a viewing today!

What I like about this ad is that, aside from giving a verbal tour of the property, it gives examples which allow the reader to imagine themselves enjoying the property as if they were there. Pair the verbal imagery with great visuals and you've got yourself an amazing advertisement. And that brings us to the next step.

Compelling Visuals

Visuals are what sets a good advertisement apart from a bad one. Browse through a bunch of rental ads and you'll clearly see the ones taken by a professional, where the photos are sharp, take in a whole room and the colors just pop. Then there are the ones taken with a cell phone in portrait orientation. They're blurry and show only a corner of a room. Not only do the latter type of photos imply a lack of professionalism, they also imply to the reader that the owner may not know what they're doing, which is not the mindset on which you want to start a prospective tenant. Your ad is your first impression to a prospective tenant, and you want it to be a good one.

Hire a professional to get some good photos. Yes, you will have to pay for them, but you only have to pay once, and you'll have photos you can use over and over again. They'll be sharp, well-composed and edited to capture the best your property has to offer. It's an investment worth every dollar. If you're tight on cash, a cell phone will still do in a pinch, but make sure it has a good camera. A lot can still be said about composition – i.e. how a photo is framed, lighting, etc. This is where a professional eye still comes in handy.

If you really want to up your game, get a video done of your property. Nothing tells a better story than a well-shot video paired with some awesome music. This can singlehandedly replace both your written ad and your photographs. If recent real-estate ads are any indication, videos are definitely the wave of the future and you can be sure to stand out from your competition this way.

Lastly, you can create a virtual tour of your property so people can walk through your house online. A 3D rendering is made of the interior of your house and it will allow whoever is viewing it to click around and walk through your property. It's not as good as actually being there but it's the next best thing, and if they still show up to see it in person then you know they're serious. In that sense, it's a great filtering tool, as well.

Tenant Screening

Now that you've gotten some tenant applications from your awesome advertisement, it's time to figure out who's naughty or nice. This is probably the most important step you can take to ensure you have less headaches down the road, so it's important to be very thorough here.

Some of the following steps may even feel like overkill, but one rotten tenant can really ruin your year, so anything to prevent that from happening is worthwhile.

Tenant Screening Checklist

Before the showing:

- ☐ **Email Tenant a questionnaire** with some preliminary questions to assess whether they're a good fit for your property. Only schedule a viewing if they're serious enough to return the questionnaire; otherwise, you're wasting your time. This is a great filtering tool. My questionnaire questions are as follows:

    o   Where did you hear about our place?
    o   Please tell me a little about yourself:
    o   What is your preferred move in date?
    o   How long do you want to rent for?

- How long have you been living at the place you are now?
- What is the reason you're looking to move?
- How many people will be living at the rental?
- Do you smoke or vape?
- Have you given notice to your current landlord?
- What's your source of income? Full-time? Part-time?
- Average monthly take-home income?
- Do you have pets? If so, how many?
- The Security Deposit is the same as one month's rent and is due before you move in. Do you foresee any problems with this?
- We do credit checks as part of our screening process, any concerns or anything we should know?

☐ **Phone or text prospect one hour before viewing** to make sure they will be there. This is to ensure you don't waste your time going to the property only to wait and have them not show up.

☐ **Do the showing and send them an application form to fill out.**

After receiving the completed application form, perform the following preliminary checks:

☐ **Call current place of employment** to verify their employment. IMPORTANT: Do not call the number listed on the application form if you can help it. Instead, Google the company the tenant says they work for and call their HR department directly. Employers are usually wary about giving out wages, so instead confirm that:

    a) the person in question works there, and
    b) the person is in a long-term position and in good standing.

Do this for every working member in the household who will be contributing to rent.

- ☐ **Call current landlord** to ask about problems with tenant in the past, history of late rents, the state in which they left their previous rental and what the landlord was charging them.

- ☐ **Call previous landlord.** If the current landlord is saying good things to get them out of his/her hair, the previous landlord should have no problems telling you the truth.

- ☐ **Search for prospect on social media** to dive a little deeper. Search their name on Facebook, Instagram, and Twitter. This gives you some idea what they do in their off-time and is a good way to find out any lies they may have told you. E.g. smoker, has a pet, party animals, etc.

Assuming the preliminary checks don't turn up any issues, ask the prospect to send the following documents. Get these documents from every employed individual in the household who will be contributing to rent:

- ☐ **Employment letter.**

- ☐ **Two (2) most current paystubs.**

- **Credit report:** This is to ensure they are not in the habit of missing payments and do not have a large amount of debt payments which may hinder them from making their rent. Ask the tenant to go to creditkarma.ca to get their credit score and report for free. Be mindful if they just send you a screenshot of their credit score as these can be easily doctored. Make sure they send you their full report as well so you can see the whole picture.

- **Copy of photo ID:** This is to ensure they are who they say they are and as a precaution against identity theft.

More checks:

- **Calculate their Gross Debt Service (GDS).** Add up the rent and utility costs the tenant has to pay and divide that by their total monthly gross income. This number ideally should be 35% or less.
    a) E.g. Monthly income is $10,000. Monthly rent is $2,000. Monthly utilities are approximately $300. Total cost of housing is approximately $2,300/month.

$2,300/$10,000 = 0.23 = 23%. 23% < 35% = GOOD!

- **Calculate their Total Debt Service (TDS).** Look at their credit report and add up all the debt payments they have to make per month. Add that number to their GDS and divide by their monthly gross income. This number ideally should be 42% or less.

- [ ] **Gut Check.** What is your gut telling you about the prospect? If something still feels off about the prospect but you can't quite tell what it is, decline the prospect. There is a good chance your subconscious mind noticed something off about the prospect that your conscious mind didn't, and it is trying to warn you. Better safe than sorry. There will always be another prospect.

If everything above checks out and you have no concerns:

- [ ] **Contact the tenant.** Email or phone the tenant to inform them that they've been approved for the rental and confirm move-in date.

- [ ] **Request payment.**
    a) If the move-in is within two weeks, ask for both the security deposit and first month's rent in the form of a certified cheque, money order, or e-transfer the day you sign the lease.
    b) If the move-in is more than two weeks away, ask for the security deposit in the form of a certified cheque, money order, or e-transfer and then they may pay their first month's rent in the agreed-upon format when they move in.

- ☐ **Schedule the move-in inspection.** Ideally schedule it within a week before the tenant moves in, though it can be scheduled sometime during the week after they've moved in (not ideal, as they may cause damage during the move-in which won't be documented). Take LOTS of pictures during the inspection. Ensure pictures are time stamped. Include tenants in pictures to prove they were present during the inspection.

- ☐ **Bring gifts.** On inspection day and upon handing over of keys, arrive early and have a gift bag ready for the new tenant. This can be some cleaning and household supplies along with a bottle of wine, some chocolates, a welcome card and some Tim Horton's or Starbucks gift-cards. You want to give them something with which to celebrate their new home and start off the tenant-landlord relationship on the right foot.

That's it! I know it seems like a lot of work, but this is the best way to ensure you have a great tenant and the most headache-free landlord experience possible.

***There are tenant checking services available as well if you don't want to do all the work and don't mind paying someone to do some of the legwork. Naborly.com is actually a service that gives you some good info on your prospective tenant and tenantverification.ca is another great service for Canadians. The services are great to give you a head start but they may not be as thorough so if you use them, it's still important for you to follow up with your own investigation. They don't do anything you wouldn't be able to do on your own and more importantly, you will give way more shits than one random person calling another random person on the phone. Just saying.

Moving Tenants In

As mentioned in the Checklist above, the best time to perform the move-in inspection is *before* they actually move in. The pictures are important in order to prove the damage or lack thereof was already present prior to move-in. This protects both you and the tenant in the event of a disagreement. In addition to the pictures, a move-in/move-out inspection checklist should be filled out and signed by both the landlord/agent and the tenant to note and agree on the current condition of the property. You can often pick up copies of the inspection checklists complete with carbon copies at your local Residential Tenancy Board Office or you can download a free copy at cwho.ca. Once the inspection is complete, ensure your tenant gets a copy via carbon copy, email or some other format.

That's it! Congratulations, you got your first tenant! Now we'll move onto the actual management of your tenant.

My Experience with Finding Tenants

Getting a property filled is arguably the hardest part of the whole rental process. Between running around for the showings, checking references and doing the inspections, this is probably most work you'll do until you have to get the vacancy filled the next time. Couple this with the stress of having an empty property and a mortgage payment lurking around the corner and many landlords may feel pressured into renting to the first tenant they come across, even though they may not be a good fit.

I have one piece of advice for this: DON'T RUSH IT!!!

Remember that reserve fund I told you to set up and set aside? One of the biggest reasons for that reserve fund is so you can take your time to find a good tenant. If it takes you a month, then it takes you a month. Sure, you have to make a mortgage payment, but that will seem like peanuts when you have to deal with a deadbeat tenant not paying rent and trashing your rental. You're going to have to deal with the cost of getting a judgement against your tenant, hiring a bailiff to kick them out, dealing with missed rent, any tenant damages, the ridiculous amount of time it takes to get this done (which may include missing work) and the sleepless nights. Trust me when I say it's worth it to wait until you find someone you like. I learned this the hard way, so I'm doing my best to make sure others don't make the same mistake.

Be thorough when doing your tenant checks. Either do it properly or hire someone to do it properly. Don't be lazy with this step or you will find yourself working a lot harder later on.

Next Actionable Step

As a thank you for getting this far in the book, visit us at www.cwho.ca and sign up for your free account to have access to copies of our tenant application, tenant screening checklist, move-in inspection forms and more for no additional charge.

You're welcome!

CHAPTER 10

TENANT MANAGEMENT

One day, a farmer went to check on the nest of his Goose and found the Goose had laid a heavy, yellow, glittering egg. Thinking it was a prank, the farmer almost threw it away, but upon further inspection, he discovered the egg was made of pure gold!

The farmer took it to the market and sold the egg for a large sum of money. Day after day, the Goose laid a single golden egg, and the farmer eventually became rich by selling the eggs. As the farmer got richer, the greedier he got, and became impatient that the Goose only laid a single golden egg a day. The farmer was not getting rich fast enough.

One day, an idea occurred to the farmer. Maybe if he cut open the Goose, he would be able to get all the gold inside at once! Shortly after, he gutted the poor thing, only to find it was just like any other goose inside – a lot of squishy parts but no gold. Now the Goose was dead, and the farmer no longer enjoyed the daily addition to his wealth.

You may have heard this story in one form or another over the years, but in every story, the moral is the same: *Don't be a dick to your Goose.*

When real estate investors think of an asset, the first thing that comes to mind is the property they own. When you look up the definition of *asset*, you get:

"Something valuable that an entity owns, benefits from or has use of in generating income."
In a way, a rental property can be considered an asset, in that you can use it to generate income. But the income doesn't come from the property. It comes from the tenants. The property on its own is technically a liability. The definition of a *liability* is as follows:

"Obligations of a company or organization. Amounts owed to lenders and suppliers."

On its own, the property, with its mortgage payments, property taxes, utilities and maintenance costs will eat you alive if left empty. That being said, the asset is not the property. The real asset is the tenant you get to live there and pay you rent. The tenant is your Golden Goose and the rental property is just a very nice barn in which to keep your Goose happy.

Rather than property management, the more appropriate term should be *Tenant Management*. You are managing the wants, needs and expectations of your tenants in order to keep them happy and pay you rent every month. Keeping your tenants happy should be your number one priority as a rental housing provider, because an empty barn does you no good.

To Manage or Not to Manage (Yourself)

This is a question many newer investors ask themselves, but there should not even be a debate. New investors should *always* manage their first couple of properties themselves. There are several good reasons for this:

1. **No one will care more than you.** Let's face it, no one will care about your rental property and your tenants more than you do. To a management company, you're just another item on a to-do list. To you, making this property work could mean *everything*, so you tell me who will put in more effort.

2. **Learn the ropes.** By managing your own property, you will learn what it takes to do it well and really appreciate the effort it takes to do a good job. This is vital when and if you eventually hire out the management, to assess whether who you hire is doing a good job.

3. **Time.** At the beginning, you'll still have a lot of it, so may as well use that time productively to learn the ins and outs of your business.

When to Hire Out Management

You should think about hiring out the management when the

time you spend on your properties can be better spent elsewhere. For example, if you're spending a lot of time on your properties rather than performing higher-return activities such as attracting investors, then you should hire someone else to manage. The bottom line is to hire management if self-managing is preventing you from doing activities which can grow your business.

Build Rapport with Your Tenants

Landlords, a.k.a. Rental Housing Providers, have gotten a bad rap over the years, so it's important to break that stereotype from the beginning. Make sure you set the expectations of your relationship up front, such as each party's responsibilities regarding the property (e.g. who changes the light bulbs, unplugs the toilet, lawncare, etc.) so there won't be any misunderstandings down the road. A move-in gift is always a good way to start things off. If your tenants have a complaint or an issue with the property, address it *immediately*.

Remember, the tenants are your Golden Geese, so you want to keep them happy so they will continue to lay those rent cheques month after month.

In short, think of every stereotype of a typical slumlord—such as not addressing tenant complaints in a timely manner, being a mean asshole, harassing tenants for rent, always wearing a tank-top with a mustard stain – and then do the complete opposite. You want to shower them with gifts on holidays, address their every concern and be as nice as you can to them.

You may be thinking that if you try to address their every concern, you'll be spending a lot of time dealing with complaints, but that's not true. If you picked your tenants well and treat them with respect, they will in turn respect your time and will rarely complain unless it's actually important. Treat them how you would want to be treated.

Keeping the Good Ones

A great tenant is a rare and amazing thing. You want to hang onto the good ones for as long as possible. This is especially important in a down market where tenants have a ton of choices when it comes to rentals. In addition to being the best landlord ever, here are some other tactics you can use to keep the good ones:

1. **Keep rents competitive.** You have to constantly make sure your rents are comparable to similar products on the market. If you're too expensive, no matter how good your services, they *will* move.

2. **Catch them early.** Approach your tenants three months before the lease is due to ask them if they're interested in renewing their lease. The idea is to catch them before they start looking because once that happens, you've potentially lost them.

3. **Offer incentives.** Give them something to renew their lease with you for another year. This is especially important when vacancies are high, and the renter has a lot of choices. A cash rebate (e.g. $500) is a good option. It's hard to say no to $500 cash-in-hand to sign a lease they were most likely going to sign anyway. If $500 seems excessive, just compare it to how much money you'd lose if the

rental stayed empty for a month.

4. **Gifts.** How many landlords do you know who give their tenants gifts on a regular basis? Exactly. Drop off a gift for birthdays (you did get a copy of their ID right?), Christmas, and even for your regular inspections. They're paying you thousands of dollars every year. You can afford to give them a $20 Starbucks gift card every now and then. You want them to be so grateful they will never want to leave.

These tactics should be part of how you operate on a regular basis, but it's even more important when the economy is down, and vacancies are high. When the tenants have many choices, you need some way to make yourself stand out from the crowd.

Getting Rid of the Bad Apples

You hear bad tenant stories all the time. One classic is, "My friend had a tenant who didn't pay rent. It took her three months to get them out and the place was completely trashed when they left."

Another is, "I know someone whose tenants started a grow-op in their basement and totally ruined the house."

This doesn't have to be you. By setting a high standard when you're screening your tenants, you can weed out most of the bad ones. Stay in this business long enough, however, and you will inevitably come across some less-desirable tenants. But it's not as hard to deal with as you think. The key here is to not let things lapse when you encounter an issue. For example, if the tenants are late on rent, serve them a 14-day notice right away. Just tell them it's standard protocol and it's nothing personal. If they pay within the 14 days, then the notice is null and void. If they don't pay, however, then you can get the eviction process started. This process varies by province, so please consult your province's Residential Tenancy Board for more details.

Problems arise when you let things slide. Getting rid of a tenant isn't hard, but it does take time for the legal process to work, and every day you let go by without taking action to kick out a bad tenant is another day of lost rent you may never get back. In Alberta, it can take a couple weeks to schedule a hearing and then the tenants are given another week or two to leave if it's in the landlord's favor, so the earlier you get started, the earlier you can find a better tenant.

The bottom line in dealing with bad tenants — act promptly.

Managing My Tenants

I do my best to start my relationships with my tenants on the best foot possible. On their move-in inspection, I give them a gift bag with some household and cleaning supplies, a bottle of champagne or wine, a box of chocolates, a gift card and a hand-written card to congratulate them on their new home. If you're lazy, there are companies such as The Little Helpers (visit www.littlehelpers.ca) where they have gift baskets you can order online and have delivered to your tenants with a personal note. What you give doesn't really matter, as long as you give something to show you care. The impression most tenants have is that their landlords don't give a crap about them, so it's our job to change that perspective. Having your tenants think you're awesome doesn't hurt, either.

On top of the move-in gifts, I send them gift cards over the holidays and maybe a bottle of wine or box of chocolates every time I do an inspection. I'm also very prompt at resolving any tenant complaints.

The goal is to make them feel as if you have their best interests at heart. The standards out there are so low, it really doesn't take much. The happier the tenant, the less they bother me, which improves the chances they'll stay for another year.

Everybody wins.

Next Actionable Step

Even though you may be managing your own properties at first, it's good to get an idea of what property management firms are in your area and what rates they charge. Give three firms a call, determine their rates, read their reviews and decided which one is the best so you know who to call when the time comes.

CHAPTER 11

JOINT VENTURES

On the show Shark Tank, hopeful and bright-eyed entrepreneurs come on stage to pitch a small group of wealthy investors an idea they think will make them millions. These entrepreneurs often need some funding to get their project off the ground in exchange for a slice of their business. Some ideas are good, and many are cringe-worthy, but occasionally, a great idea comes along which will have the Sharks jumping at the opportunity to invest.

One particularly memorable episode had two guys pitching a new drone design where it went from vertical take-off to horizontal propulsion, allowing the drone to fly at speeds several times faster than anything on the market. The potential was enormous for everything from military applications to a new era of cinematography. Not only did these entrepreneurs get a deal, but it turned into a bidding war where they got three times more than what they'd asked for and got every Shark in on the deal in exchange for 20% of the business.

This, my friend, is an example of a joint venture.

Joint ventures, in many ways, are the lifeblood of real estate investing. Your own money can only go so far. You can save your ass off, eat nothing but instant noodles and wear the same clothes until they're rags for a couple of years, all to buy one investment property. That is great and admirable, but if you want to build a real estate portfolio faster, you're going to need some help. That's where joint-venture partnerships come in.

Joint ventures may sound like a big, scary business word, but all it really means is joining forces with someone else to combine your resources in order to achieve a goal or purchase an investment which neither of you could accomplish alone. For example, Jimmy just turned 10 years old and got $200 in birthday money. He really wants a PlayStation 4 that costs $400 but his parents refuse to pay the difference. Instead of just being mad at his parents for ruining his childhood, Jimmy got creative. He called up his classmate Jason and asked if he wanted to pitch in the other $200 and they would have shared custody of the game system. Jimmy wrote up a little agreement that they would exchange custody of the PS4 every month, with the option to buy out the other partner at any time. They enjoyed this agreement for a year-- until Jimmy's 11th birthday, when he got enough money to buy Jason out.

Real estate is no different, and it's more common than you probably think. Most successful investors became successful because of their joint-venture relationships, and any major development you see requires the use of joint-venture investors. If you're planning on making real estate investing a business, joint venturing becomes a necessity. Similar to the way an entrepreneur on Shark Tank needs investment money to keep growing, so does your real estate investing business.

When you're soliciting joint-venture money to fund your investment, it may seem hard because it can feel as if you are begging for money. You are not begging for money. Let's repeat that again. *You are not begging for money.* As an investor and entrepreneur, you are offering opportunities and solving problems. It's important to reframe the concept in your mind that you are offering your investors an opportunity to invest with you and profit with you. No one is profiting at the expense of the other. You both need each other in order to take full advantage of a profitable opportunity. The real estate expert provides the deal and manages the property while the money partner provides the necessary capital to move the project forward. By thinking of an investment this way, it makes it a lot easier to approach your friends or family with a deal and make your case. Your investors also aren't dumb. They'll be able to tell whether or not you have a good deal on your hands. Your job is to explain to them why you think it's a good deal and they'll take it from there.

My Growth Story

I bought my first rental property in 2013 with my own money. Even though I was working at the time, I was living like a student and renting a studio apartment in order to save up enough to make a down payment. In three years' time, I had $30,000 saved up, but I still needed another $50,000 in order to make a 20% down payment. Even though it was my first house, I really didn't want to pay the $14,000 in mortgage insurance at the time for a $400k home, so I calculated how much it would cost to borrow $50,000 instead. My dad had a home equity line of credit he wasn't using, so I asked if I could borrow from that and pay it off on my own. He agreed. I figured as long as I could pay it off in less than nine years, the interest would still be less than what they would charge for the insurance--so that's exactly what I did. I actually managed to pay it off in three years. In 2014, I joined forces with my sister and a couple of cousins and picked up another rental property where we each put up one quarter of the down payment. I didn't know what a joint venture was at the time, but that's essentially what we were doing. I did one more two years later with another family member where we each put down 50% of the down payment. By this point, however, I was pretty much out of money and my lines of credit were maxed out. I wanted to keep growing, but I felt stuck. Fortunately, my real estate education and experience had gotten to the point where I felt confident in my skills as a managing partner and was able to find friends and family who became my money partners through the next several deals. I'm happy to say it's been going strong ever since.

The hardest part for me in this transition from a solopreneur to an entrepreneur raising funds was reframing my mindset from asking for money to offering an opportunity. It took a while, and along the way, I worked for free and gave up a lot of my time and advice for little-to-no compensation. Granted, many of my investors were family and friends, so I didn't mind, but I also didn't place enough value on my time and expertise. The validation I've gotten since then from successful deals I've put together have helped me get over that limiting mindset. I haven't turned into a bloodsucking parasite charging my investors for every second of advice, but I've come to realize the value I can provide, and don't mind asking for compensation when the work I put in is justified. For some more good education on joint-venture partnerships in real estate, I found the book **Real Estate Joint Ventures: the Canadian Investor's Guide to Raising Money and Getting Deals Done** to be a really good resource. I'm not getting paid to say this, and the cover makes it look like the least interesting book you'll never want to read, but it was a solid book on the topic.

Next Actionable Step

Give **Real Estate Joint Ventures** a good read and then have a conversation with your friends and family to gauge their interest in real estate. Don't be pushy. You're not making a sale or anything. You just want to see whether real estate is an area of interest to them and make a mental note of any potential joint-venture partners when you come across your next good deal. You want to tell, not sell.

CHAPTER 12

TREATING IT LIKE A BUSINESS

In 1940, two brothers, Richard and Maurice, opened a little drive-in burger shack near Pasadena, California. The restaurant was doing well enough, but by 1948, they realized their eatery could be more profitable if they increased efficiency by streamlining the menu and preparing food ahead of rush times.

By 1955, the brothers had already franchised six restaurants before meeting a milkshake machine salesman by the name of Ray Kroc. With Ray's help, the brothers expanded their franchise to 228 locations over the next five years, grossing $56 million dollars annually by 1960.

Fast forward to today, and McDonald's is the world's largest restaurant chain by revenue, serving more than 69 million people daily in over 100 countries and generating over $22.8

billion dollars in yearly revenue.

To open a McDonald's requires a startup cost of $1 million to $2.2 million dollars and the franchisee has to pay the franchise as much as 16% of their gross revenue in fees and rent every month. Sixteen percent of gross! That's a lot of money. And yet between 2014 and 2017, they grew their number of restaurants by a staggering 983 locations. The strength of McDonald's and their continued growth comes from their systems. Everything in a McDonald's, from how they assemble their burgers down to the machines they use, are designed to get food to the counter as efficiently as possible. More than anything, it's this system for which the franchisees are paying. Their systems and processes are what makes McDonald's so successful.

Similarly, it's systems and processes which will take your real estate game to the next level.

Many new landlords treat their rental property like an afterthought or a hobby. They buy one as an investment but deal with issues ad hoc as they come up and don't take the necessary steps a business owner needs to take in order for their business to thrive, or at the very least, to operate efficiently. Before you think anything else--*yes*, your rental property is a business.

You have a product (housing), customers (tenants), it generates income (rent) and has operating expenses similar to any business. To really grow your real estate business, or any business, for that matter, you have to think about designing it from the beginning like a franchise. By creating systems which allow scalability and outsourcing of repetitive work, it greatly reduces the stress of running the business and significantly improves the chance of it surviving in the long-term.

Some people may say they only plan to have a couple of rentals so they don't see the point of creating all these systems and processes because they don't plan to grow and it would just be a waste of effort. The point of systems and processes is to improve the efficiency of a business by determining specific roles within the business so that when a business grows, people can be brought in to fill those roles. Even someone with one or two properties can benefit from this. Say you want to go on holiday but need a vacancy filled. If you've created a checklist on how to screen tenants and do the walkthrough, then you can give this checklist to a friend and be assured he will work in a similar way. If nothing else, treating your rentals like a business can free up your time, allowing you to do the things in life which really matter. The whole purpose of real estate is to generate a source of passive income to fund the life you want to live, so the ultimate goal should be to extract yourself from the system as much as possible.

So, what does *systems and scalability* actually mean when it comes to the business of real estate? Let's go through these in more detail.

Systems

Put simply, a business system is a procedure, process, method or course of action designed to achieve a specific result. The results should be repeatable, measurable and consistent. Any step in a business which is regularly repeated can be incorporated as part of a system. In rental real estate, areas you can systematize include tenant screening, advertising, property analysis and basically anything repeated on a regular basis. Creating systems allows you to more easily outsource your tasks to others, freeing up your time to do more important work, such as raising money from investors or whatever else would move the business forward. It's basically a manual to train others to do exactly what you have done to ensure results are on par and consistent. The most beautiful thing about creating systems is it allows you to remove yourself from part of the machine which makes the business run, so you can be focused instead on the direction the machine is heading. It is also an important step in being able to scale your business.

Scaling or Scalability

Scaling a business means being able to maintain the same level of performance and efficiency in your business under an ever-expanding workload. What this means in your real estate business is ideally to be able to provide the same standard of service to one tenant and one property as you can to 10 properties and even 100 properties. Creating systems is an important first step. The next step is to outsource those repetitive tasks to others with the systems you designed so you can focus on more high-value activities.

When you first start your business, having a business structure in mind is a good place to start, so you know which roles have to be replaced when your business grows and you need to hire people to occupy those roles. Below is an example of one such structure:

When you first start out, you may find you're the one filling all of the roles, such as Property Manager, Marketing Director and Bookkeeper. There's nothing wrong with that if you have just one or two properties and it's still manageable. In fact, doing all those jobs is a good idea in the beginning as it gives you an idea of what the expectations of these roles are so you'll know what to look for when you hire into those positions. However, if you want to grow, keeping yourself in those roles becomes counterproductive as it takes time away from more important tasks, such as finding investors and

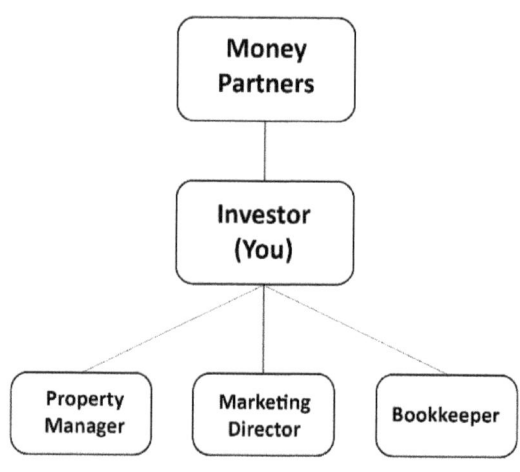

managing those relationships. To be able to scale properly, you have to be able to delegate less-important tasks. The key word here is *delegate*, not abdicate. You still have to manage the managers, but delegating leaves you more time to focus on what you do best.

The ultimate goal here is to free up more time. That is the reason we started all this, right? To generate semi-passive income so we have more time to do the things which make us happy.
For you, this can mean taking more time to grow your business or go travelling. Whatever that thing may be, you can't do it when you're doing a half-a-dozen jobs at once. So, find someone capable, train them well and delegate appropriately.

Some people ask when is the best time to outsource our responsibilities, as some don't see a point when they only have one or two properties. A good rule of thumb is this--if your management tasks are taking time away from activities which move you closer to your ultimate goal, then it's time to outsource.

Be a Professional

Being a professional means checking your emotions at the door. This is especially important when dealing with problem tenants or tenants who pay with sob stories instead of cash. If you ran a store, you would not tolerate someone stealing from you. In real estate, your product is the shelter you provide. Anyone not paying their rent is essentially stealing, and this behaviour should not be tolerated. There are no shortages of sob stories. This doesn't mean you should not be compassionate and hear them out, but in the end, the mortgage isn't going to pay itself, so you have to either find a tenant who can pay or you fork out the bill yourself. Don't be a jerk about it but be firm when it comes to enforcing your rental policies and making clear to the tenant what the consequences are.

My Systems and Processes

At this point, I have 16 rental units and I still manage them myself. When I had just a couple of units, it wasn't a lot of work. I composed emails and created documents as they were required. However, as I accumulated more units, I found this ad hoc approach took up increasingly more time. I eventually decided that creating some standardized documents up front would save me a lot more time in the long run. The benefit isn't just in the time savings alone. By having steps someone else can follow to achieve the same results, you can now outsource your work to someone else and expect them to do almost as good a job as you. I say *almost* because no one will care for your properties as much as you. But as long as the results are acceptable, you have to be okay with that in order to grow.

I've included an example of a letter template I send to my prospective rental tenants after I review their application form and decide they have potential and need more information to finish my due diligence:

> Hey_____,
>
> *Thank you for submitting your application. I am pleased to inform you that after reviewing your application, you are conditionally approved for the rental at _____.*

In order for us to complete the application, we will need a copy of the following documents as soon as possible:

- *Current employment letter*
- *Most recent 2 paystubs*
- *Current credit report*
- *Photocopy of your driver's license*

If you have any questions or concerns, please don't hesitate to contact me.

Kindest regards,

Phil Wong

Whenever I get to this stage of the rental process, I just type in the name and address and press send. Easy and done.

Not only is this useful for operating a business, but anything repetitive in your life may benefit from creating a system in order to improve efficiency.

Next Actionable Step

Find at least one thing in your life you do repetitively and create a system for it so it will be easier or more efficient every time you have to perform that task again in the future. It could be an email you often send out or having a specific place to put your car keys every time you come home so you're not scrambling to find them when you're rushing to leave your house last minute the next morning.

CHAPTER 13

WHAT IF...

Anxiety often results from not knowing what will happen in the future. That uncertainty triggers fear, which leads to a fight-or-flight response. If you're new at real estate investing, there are bound to be some unknowns. Sometimes the fear of those unknowns is enough to paralyze someone from moving forward. There is no such thing as zero risk when it comes to--well-- anything. Even a chunk of cash sitting in a savings account making 2% a year runs the risk of depreciating, because it's not keeping up with inflation. You can, however, mitigate risk. This chapter should give you the tools to prepare for the most common issues related to real estate investing and hopefully alleviate some of those unknowns and the fear associated with them so you don't shit your bed at night thinking about your new investment.

What if the Tenants Don't Pay?

Thoroughly screening your tenants is the best way to prevent yourself from letting undesirables live in your property. Ensure you check all their references, credit reports and employment verification. By ensuring they have adequate income and are responsible with their money, you can greatly reduce the chances they won't pay. Refer to Chapter 8 for the detailed checklist.

Secondly, be prompt with your 14-day eviction notices and other paperwork if paying on time is a problem. By being timely with your paperwork, you reduce the time it takes to get rid of a bad tenant and reduce the risk of additional lost income. Refer to Chapter 10 for a more detailed description on getting rid of bad apples.

What if My Tenant Trashes the Property?

Make sure you call their previous landlord to see if they had any issues and search your tenants on social media to see if there is any evidence of them being party animals. The best way to protect yourself from this is to ensure you have tenant damage protection. A number of insurance companies can add this protection to your policy, so ask around. It may add to your premium but will save you a lot of sleepless nights.

What if the Property Doesn't Rent?

For the right price, anything will rent. To improve your chances of it renting faster, make sure your rents are in line with the market. Google the most popular rental sites in your area to research rents. Padmapper.com compiles all the online listings of rentals in your area, so it's a good place to start to get an idea of what you should be charging for your property. Rentfaster.com, Kijiji.com, Facebook Marketplace, and Craigslist are also good sites for researching rents in your area. Having your property look better than comparable properties in the area will also help it rent faster, so consider things like curb appeal, finishings, appliances, flooring and paint. If it's a place you'd want to live, others will likely feel the same.

What if the Housing Market Drops?

History has shown over a long enough period of time, real estate has only appreciated in value. Nevertheless, you still have to be mindful of your purchase and focus on the fundamentals of an area (see Chapter 6) to maximize your chances of making a good purchase. If the math works--if it is a positive cashflow property which meets all of your parameters in the current market, then it's a good buy. If the market goes up, awesome. But if it drops, then at least you have a property which can keep itself alive until things recover.

What if Interest Rates go Up?

As with the housing market, it's also difficult to guess where interest rates will go, but as of the writing of this book, interest rates are just coming out of historic lows and are slowly going up. When doing the expense calculations (see Chapter 6) on your property before you buy, use higher interest rates in your math to stress-test your property. This will give you an idea of how high interest rates have to go before you run into issues. If you find your investment can't stand a bit of an interest hike before the cashflow goes negative, then maybe it's not a great buy in the first place.

What if Rent Control gets Implemented?

Some provinces, such as Alberta and Saskatchewan, are lucky in that there are no provincial rent-control policies in place. This means those provinces can raise rents as much as they want once every 365 days. The other provinces aren't so lucky. If you're in one of these provinces, just make sure to take advantage of the allowed rent increases every year if the market allows and to bump the rent for new tenants. Others have made it work, so there's no reason you can't, as well.

What if My Rent Doesn't Cover My Expenses?

This one's easy. Don't buy it.

What if the Property Ends Up Vacant for Several Months Between Tenants?

This scenario is a very real possibility, but again, there are a few ways to mitigate this loss. The LAST thing you want to do is approve a tenant because you're desperate and not because they're actually a good fit. This is the most common reason for headaches, sleepless nights and tenant horror stories. There are a few ways to prevent this:

1. **Keep a slush fund in your property's account.** It's a good idea to keep at least three months of mortgage payments in your property's account in the event the property sustains a prolonged vacancy. This way you know you have at least three months to find a tenant before shit starts

hitting the fan, so can take your time and find the right tenant. This slush fund can either come from holding onto the monthly cashflow and letting that build up or factoring the cost into the property at the beginning when you buy, so you can sleep soundly from the get-go.

2. **Lower your rent to get someone in faster.** This isn't ideal, especially if you're losing money, but if it's a slow market, this may be the best way to cut your losses. For example, you lower your rent to $1,300 a month, but it is negative $100 every month. Sure, you'll lose $1,200 over the course of the year, but it's still better than the $1,300 for an extra month of vacancy. If you were cashflow positive before the slump, those times will come back. You just have to be patient. Again, that's what a slush fund is for.

3. **Offer incentives.** A free month of rent, a free TV, free Internet for six months or free housekeeping. Do something to make your property stand out from the crowd.

What if Different Tenants in a Property don't get Along?

This is a common issue if you have a property with more than one rental unit, such as a suited house with a tenant upstairs and another in the basement, or an apartment complex with multiple tenants in a building. The issues could be anything from fighting over the use of common spaces to parking issues, but the most common issue tends to be noise complaints. In these situations, it's important for you to hear each tenant out and act as a mediator to find a solution or compromise with which both parties are happy.

For example, I had a basement tenant who, despite my best efforts in adding sound insulation, complained about the upstairs tenant's kids making too much noise in the evening when they ran around. The upstairs tenants, in turn, complained about the basement tenant playing her music too loud and the bass coming through the vents. I listened to each party's concerns and then asked each party to agree to one condition we negotiated together. The upstairs tenant had their children play on the second floor after 9 p.m. and the downstairs tenant turned off the bass when playing her music. It helped that they generally liked each other and there have been no further issues since. The important thing here is to be mindful and compassionate about everyone's needs. However, if there's one tenant who's disturbing the peace for everyone, that should be enough to constitute a breach of contract and you can kick them out.

CHAPTER 14

BRINGING IT ALL TOGETHER

Real estate is a broad and deep topic. You can read a dozen books and not cover it all. With stocks in the stock market, you can buy-and-hold long-term, do calls, puts, futures, shorts, derivatives, and any number of things to make money. Real estate is no different. There are buy-and-holds, rent-to-owns, assignments, flips, development, hard-money lending, joint ventures, farmland, and the list goes on and on.

This book focuses on *buy-and-hold* for a couple of reasons. First of all, it is the easiest for new investors to understand because many people are already familiar with buying and holding onto a house if they have a personal residence. Secondly, *buy-and-hold* has been shown to be the best method to create long-term, generational wealth. If you have the patience and the time, nothing beats *buy-and-hold* when it comes to long-term returns.

The thing that holds back many people from taking action toward the life they want is the thing staring back at them in the mirror every morning. It's *you*. More specifically, it's the fear and anxiety living inside you. It's that voice of self-doubt in the back of your mind that whisper the *"what if"* and *"you can't"* in its sweet, sultry Morgan Freeman voice, lulling you into a placid state of ambivalence. Those well-meaning friends and family who tell you to stick to your day job and live the safe life rather than pursuing your dreams, because if you give up, they feel justified in giving up on their own dreams for the safe comfort of anonymous oblivion. Do not give in to those voices. Instead, listen to the voice that's telling you there is more to this life than what they teach you in school. There is more to this life than what your friends and family are trying to get you to believe. The problem with school is that it teaches us failure has consequences. When you fail a test or assignment and get a poor grade, that grade pulls down your average and negatively impacts your final grade at the end of the year. Doing poorly in school could seriously affect your prospects of getting into areas of higher education, where marks matter.

What school *doesn't* teach us—and is one of the most important of real life's lessons, is when you fail at something in real life, the consequences are often minimal. On the contrary, failing something in real life is generally when you learn the most. You're more likely to succeed the next time around. Thomas Edison had over 9000 failed lightbulb experiments, but he simply saw those as 9000 options that didn't work, narrowing down the options he had toward something that would work.

This is not to say that **ALL** failures don't have consequences.

An FBI negotiator failing to defuse a hostage situation can have things go south with some major consequences. For most of us mere mortals and entrepreneurs however, the rule of the game is to fail fast and fail often.

Real estate investing is no different. As long as you do your due diligence and make sure whatever you buy is cashflow positive from Day One, the consequences are minimal and that first purchase will teach you *so much* – more than you will ever learn from reading a book or listening to podcasts. Perfect investments are very rare, and it may be many years before you come across one. Good or very good investments however, come around all the time. If it's your first investment, a good or very good investment is all you need. The value comes less from what you *make* from the investment (albeit still important) but more from what you *learn* from the investment. You'll also look more legit and can show others you can take care of business, which will improve the confidence of those investing with you.

I wrote this book in the hopes it will give you the tools and guidance you need to get started on your real estate investing journey. A journey of a thousand miles starts with a single step, and I want to thank you for taking this first step with me. Now it's up to you to take the next one.

There are no overnight success stories in real estate investing. It's not easy and it's not for the faint-hearted, but the best things in life worth doing rarely are. Start simple, focus on a niche and own it. Never stop learning, never give up and I know you can crush it.

Next Actionable Step

Go out there, have fun and make shit happen!

www.ingramcontent.com/pod-product-compliance
Ingram Content Group UK Ltd.
Pitfield, Milton Keynes, MK11 3LW, UK
UKHW021325180426
11947UKWH00017B/1445